MW00629292

*Praise for **From a Father***

"***From a Father to a Child*** *should be read by everyone, regardless of whether they are a parent or not. This book is filled with wisdom that can potentially help anyone become a greater and grander version of who they are. I felt the love and genuine concern this author feels for his family and for you, the reader. Dive in now, and enjoy an inspiring journey."*

– Peggy McColl
New York Times Best Selling Author

"*I have known Michael Johns for close to twenty years. What he shares in his new book,* **From a Father to a Child,** *is exactly how he has lived his life. God and family first, spend less than you make, take calculated risks and bet on yourself. While these are simple concepts, they are not easy to do. Mike's book provides a road map for those who choose the path less traveled, and more importantly, the gift of these concepts: a living example and a legacy for his children.*"

– Colin Braithwaite
Corporate Entrepreneur and Author of A Good Walk Unspoiled

"*I've worked with Michael both directly and indirectly for many years and if I could describe him in one word I'd say he's balanced. By balanced, I do not mean average in any way, shape or form, as he was the top-performing salesperson on our entire team. I mean he has his priorities in order, excels at them all, but is sure to not let one facet of his life overpower the other. I've personally witnessed Michael turn down opportunities for perceived career advancements because the travel requirements would impact his time with family and his ability to coach his kids. While it was a promotion on paper, it was out of balance with Michael's life goals and he had the ability to be selfless and say no. What this book will teach us all is that he was actually following his compass because he values his time with his family more than a title or the recognition our society places upon people in leadership positions. There is something in this book for us all as we each go on our own life's journey.*"

– Dan Flood
Chief Revenue Officer and Vice President of Global Sales for Pivot3

*"**From a Father to a Child** is a treasure, and absolutely required reading for anyone who values family and seeks to build a better life for themselves and pass this knowledge on to their children and grandchildren. Inspiring and heartwarming, yet packed with practical and specific steps to creating and maintaining intergenerational wealth, this book is a blueprint on how to live a life of fulfillment, success and contentment! This book will transform your life!"*

– Matthew O'Brien
Real Estate CEO, Author of **The Complete Idiot's Guide to Online Buying and Selling a Home** and *Chameleon: The March Madness Murders: A Novel* and proud father of Alice, Andrew and Evan O'Brien

FROM A
FATHER
TO A
CHILD

A Collection of Thoughts

Michael R. Johns

Hasmark
PUBLISHING
INTERNATIONAL

Published by
Hasmark Publishing
www.hasmarkpublishing.com

Copyright © 2020 Michael R. Johns
First Edition

Permission should be addressed in writing to Michael R. Johns at MichaelJohns0923@gmail.com

Editor: Kathryn Young
kathryn@hasmarkpublishing.com

Cover & Book Design: Anne Karklins
anne@hasmarkpublishing.com

ISBN 13: 978-1-989756-22-5
ISBN 10: 1989756220

To my dad,
who was so far ahead of the pack, he left footprints to follow.

And to all three of my kids – Nicholas, Hayli Rose, and Noah –
while I frequently fall short,
you provide me daily inspiration to be the best I can be.

FOREWORD

One of my favorite authors, and a "Father of Motivational and Self-Improvement" efforts, is the late Earl Nightingale. One of Nightingale's books is titled *The Strangest Secret*. At the beginning of the book, he rattles off some startling statistics about people and their financial situations.

By the age of 65:

- Only 1 out of 100 will be rich
- Only 4 out of 100 will be financially independent
- 41 out of 100 will still be working
- 54 out of 100 will be broke

He goes on to point out the following:

- We learn to read by the age of 7.
- We learn to make a living by the age of 25.
- Yet, by the age of 65, a full 40 years after we learn to make a living, we haven't learned how to be financially independent in the richest country on earth.

Why? We conform, Nightingale says. The problem is we follow, or conform to, the 95 out of 100 people who have no idea what they're doing. *It would be far better to seek out the advice and counsel of the 5 out of 100 that seem to have a good grasp on how to be successful.* If you want to emulate someone, make sure you are emulating someone in the top 5, not in the bottom 95. You'll be far better off.

Further, seek counsel from yourself. Take time to think, and then take action on the ideas you generate. These two approaches will prove to be far more effective than blindly following the herd, which is what 95 out of 100 people do.

The aim of this book is to provide the kind of information and guidance that those top 5 out of 100 successful people would give you.

I'm under no illusion that this book is an end-all, be-all answer to the secrets of the universe. I'm not that smart. However, my hope is this book is a good guide and will stimulate your thinking. Additionally, this is not just a book about wealth, although I have started with some startling facts to get you thinking and devoted an entire chapter to it. Rather, it is more about providing coaching and guidance along the following lines:

- Advice on leading a balanced life
- Tips on how to achieve your goals, and why having goals in the first place is critically important
- Discussions on right from wrong
- Definitions of a few values that I think are important

There are multiple stories, some funny/some serious, from famous people to my own experiences, to illustrate various points.

My hope is you find this book both enjoyable and informative.

Good reading…

TABLE OF CONTENTS

CHAPTER

INTRODUCTION
FATHERHOOD AND LEADERSHIP

My first child, Nicholas Michael Johns, was born on May 3, 2006, a day I will remember vividly for as long as I live. It's difficult to put into words the feelings parents have the first time they look at their first child. Only another parent could understand the feelings of love, pride, hope, and excitement. That being said, there are other feelings that cross a first-time parent's mind: nervousness, anxiety, and maybe even a little fear.

Fatherhood

Over the last few months of my wife's pregnancy, we did the normal things to prepare for his arrival. We created a nursery for him, which was more expensive than I expected. We began to buy clothes, and certainly, we received more than our fair share of gifts from family members, the customary baby shower, and items that friends and neighbors no longer needed. In the first few months of our son's life, we continued to make sure we were prepared in case anything happened to me or my wife. We reviewed our life insurance policies, updated our will, and in the tragic event something happened to both of us, we had a loving couple (my wife's aunt and uncle) lined up to care for our son.

However, even though we felt we had all of the logistical things taken care of, there is still one thing that is extremely difficult to prepare for: parenthood. There is no class to attend, precious few seminars, and our public school systems don't cover it. There are no doubt countless books written on the subject, but who's to say these people know what they're talking about.

Thus, the dilemma for me continued for many months. I continued to question myself on whether I had what it took to be a really good father. These questions continued well past the day my wife and I took our son home from the hospital. At the time of this writing, my wife and I have been blessed with two more kids (Hayli Rose and Noah). As I continued to think about what it would take to be a good father, and still do to this day, I realized I already had a pretty good blueprint—I could use my own father as a role model, a role he served exceptionally well. It's funny how sometimes in life when you are looking for answers to complex questions, the answers often end up being right in front of you.

I tend to be a bit obsessive. I set goals. I work off of to-do lists. And I always put things in writing. So true to my nature, I decided to write a book. Now, this is not a book for others on how to be a good father. As I began writing this book, my son Nicholas was just two years old, so obviously, the jury was still out on my fatherhood skills. Our three kids are now 14, 11, and 6. To this day, the jury is still out—I can tell you without hesitation being a father is a work in progress. I've made my share of mistakes along the way. That said, I've included advice from a blog at the end of this chapter on how a father can maintain a strong relationship with his son. By the way, the blog was written by a mother!

While I hope other fathers get something out of reading this, this book is primarily written for my kids. I mentioned earlier that we reviewed our will, life insurance policies, and custodial responsibilities should something happen to both my wife and me. Further, I began to get a handle on what the blueprint was to be a good father, using my own father's example as a guide.

However, the purpose of this book is if something should happen to me, I want my kids to still be able to hear my own words. I decided a book would be the most effective way for me to pass something on to them. It was important for me to be able to communicate and impart my beliefs and values to them, something I hope they can use as a guide throughout their own lives. I want to be able to communicate right from wrong, what it takes to be successful, and a whole lot more. Ultimately, I think any parent's goal for their children is they want them to be productive members of society and to be happy. The following poem is a good guide on happiness.

A Collection of Thoughts

Steps to Happiness

We Know:
You can't be all things to all people.
You can't do all things at once.
You can't do all things equally well.
You can't do all things better than everyone else.
Your humanity shows just like everyone else's.

So:
You have to find who you really are, and be that.
You have to decide what comes first, and do that.
You have to discover your strengths, and use them.
You have to learn to not always compete with others.
Because no one else is in the contest of 'being you.'

Then:
You will have learned to accept your own uniqueness.
You will have learned to set priorities and make decisions.
You will have learned to live with your limitations.
You will have learned to give yourself the respect you deserve.
And, you'll know you're a valuable, lovable individual.

Dare to Believe:
You are a wonderful, unique person.
You are a once-in-all-history event.
It's your right to be who you are.
Life is not a problem to solve, but a gift to cherish.
And you'll be able to stay one-up on what used to get you down.

Author Unknown

A Collection of Thoughts

Before we continue, I would like to comment on the subject of leadership. Somewhere along the way, I picked up a quote that has always stuck with me: *True leaders are so far ahead of the pack, they leave footprints for others to follow.*

As I thought about what fatherhood is all about, it occurred to me being a father is largely about leadership. There are several areas where leadership translates into fatherhood. The rest of this chapter looks at the essential qualities of leadership.

Leadership

How do we define leadership? One definition is the act of leading people or a group. Being a leader means to provide guidance, direction, and oversight. Leadership can be difficult to define, but you know it when you see it. Thus, I think it's easier to describe what leaders do, what you see in action, rather than to define it. So, in the following section are some observations on what leaders, and good fathers, do, including:

(1) Lead by example

(2) Communicate effectively

(3) Are principled yet flexible

(4) Inspire others

(5) Make people feel part of something special

(6) Influence others

(7) Build trust

(8) Recognize accomplishments

(9) Hold people accountable

(1) Lead by Example

One characteristic all good leaders have is they lead by example. You've no doubt heard the expression *actions speak louder than words*. Every leader I have ever been around largely sets the tone for the entire organization by their actions just as much as their words. In a professional setting, this might include being the first to arrive at the office in the morning and the last one to leave at night. In the home, this might be a husband avoiding criticizing his wife in front of the kids. Keep in mind, when the man of the house treats his wife in a disrespectful way, not only are you hurting your wife's feelings, but you are setting a bad example for your kids. Tearing your wife down in front of your kids is never a good idea.

When I worked for the Xerox Corporation early in my career, I worked for a General Manager named George Hodgson. I was a new Supervisor at the time with virtually no experience. We'd have weekly one-on-one discussions, where I'd review our team's performance with him. When it came to people, he'd talk about setting the right tone for the team, ethics, work ethic, and much more. He had a pet saying, "Make sure the original is worth copying." No pun intended.

(2) Communicate Effectively

Another characteristic of good leaders is they are highly effective communicators. This shows up in many different ways:

- Leaders listen.
- Leaders make sure what is expected is clearly communicated and understood.
- Leaders inspire you to be constantly reaching for improvement, striving to be the very best you can be.
- Leaders make certain (communicate) that when something needs to get done, people understand the what, why, and the how.
- Leaders hold people accountable when they are falling short of what is expected of them.
- Leaders ensure people know the direction of the entire organization and what each person's role is inside that direction.

Communication needs to be clear, consistent, and frequent. If you're going to err, err on the side of over-communicating, not under-communicating.

I read a funny story a number of years ago regarding the importance of communicating. It was about a judge interviewing a woman regarding her impending divorce. The story went like this:

Judge: "What are the grounds for your divorce?"
Wife: "About four acres and a nice little home in the middle of the property with a stream running by."

Judge: "No, I mean, what is the foundation for this case?"
Wife: "It is made of concrete, brick, and mortar."

Judge: "I mean, what are your relations like?"
Wife: "I have an aunt and uncle living here in town, and so do my husband's parents."

Judge: "Let me try one more time. Do you have a grudge?"
Wife: "No, we have a two-car carport and have never really needed one."

Judge: "Please. Is there any infidelity in your marriage?"
Wife: "Yes, both my son and daughter have stereo sets. We don't necessarily like the music, but the answer to your question is yes."

Judge: "Ma'am, does your husband ever beat you?"
Wife: "Yes, about twice a week, he gets up earlier than I do."

Judge: Exasperated, the judge finally asks, "Ma'am, do you want a divorce?"
Wife: "No, I don't want one at all. But my husband does. He says we have a communication problem."

Lee Iacocca, the former Chrysler CEO, wrote in his autobiography, "I only wish I could find an institute that teaches people how to listen. After all, a good manager needs to listen at least as much as he needs to talk. Too many people fail to realize that real communication goes in both directions."

The same could be said of a father... *listen at least as much as you talk*. This is a great way to get to know your kids, know what they like, find out what they are into, what type of people they are hanging around, and what makes them tick. Ask them questions, then really intently listen to their answers.

- How was your day?
- What was the funniest thing that happened at school today?
- What is your favorite subject in school?
- Why do you like to play soccer?
- Is there a boy or girl you particularly like? Why her/him?
- Who did you sit next to at lunch?

By asking questions, you're showing your kids you are genuinely interested in them. And, you are getting to know them on a very personal level at the same time.

(3) Are Principled Yet Flexible

There will be times when you have to bend a little to get things done. Our 16th President, Abraham Lincoln, displayed this throughout his presidency as he managed the Civil War. At one point during the war, Lincoln wanted Salmon Chase, Secretary of the Treasury, to issue interest-bearing currency as a way to raise money to support the Union's war effort. Chase was not comfortable doing this, as he felt it was unconstitutional. At this time, it was an unprecedented request in our nation's history. Certainly Lincoln could have ordered him to do it, but he didn't. Lincoln was a famous storyteller, and frequently used stories to get his point across and influence people toward his way of thinking.

Lincoln told Chase the story of an Italian captain who inadvertently ran his ship into a rock bed, which gashed a hole in its bottom. The captain ordered his men to begin pumping the water out of the ship's hull. While they were doing that, the captain began to pray before a Virgin Mary statue at the bow of the ship. The leak was overrunning his men's ability to pump the water out, and just as it looked like the ship might sink, the captain, in a fit of rage, grabbed the Virgin Mary statue and threw it overboard. Suddenly, the leak was shored up, the men pumped all of the water out of the hull, and the ship was sailed back to port. Upon docking for repairs, it was discovered the Virgin Mary had been stuck in the very hole that nearly sank the ship.

Chase didn't at first make the connection between this story and the request Lincoln had made. Lincoln explained, "Chase, I don't intend precisely to throw the Virgin Mary overboard, and by that, I mean the Constitution, but I will stick it in the hole if I can. These rebels are violating the Constitution in order to destroy the Union. I will violate the Constitution if necessary to save the Union. And I suspect, Chase, that our Constitution is going to have a rough time of it before we get done with this."

No doubt, Lincoln believed in the Constitution, but his first responsibility as President was to "preserve, protect, and defend the Constitution of the United States." If the Union had been defeated in the Civil War, there would no longer be a Constitution to protect and defend. Lincoln instinctively knew his first responsibility was to preserve it, at all costs, and so he did. This is a classic example of being principled yet flexible.

(4) Inspire Others

Another trait leaders exhibit is they have the ability to inspire others. How do they do that? Inspiring people is all about these five qualities:

- **Be positive—all the time.** Do you like being around negative people who complain and make excuses? Of course not. Leaders are positive people who never make excuses and take responsibility for whatever happens to them—positive or negative. Colin Powell, a former US General and Secretary of State, had a great saying, "Perpetual optimism is a force multiplier."

- **Help people focus on working toward continuous improvement.** One of the most important characteristics a person can develop is to learn that they can change their circumstances through their effort and attitude. Leaders invest one-on-one time in their people (and their kids) to help them develop themselves. People development is not an "add water and stir" proposition. It takes time. It takes resources. It takes patience.

- **Be enthusiastic.** If you leave your kids with anything, leave them with enthusiasm. Nothing significant was ever achieved in the absence of enthusiastic people. People achieve more when they know someone believes in them, and when they believe their best days are ahead of them.

- **Link effort to accomplishment.** This is kind of an if/then proposition. IF you can show people how their efforts will achieve a certain goal, THEN there will be a payoff at the end. And of course, it always makes sense to recognize the actual accomplishment publicly. I saw this first-hand with a team I was leading early in my career. Back in 1994, I was an onsite Operations Manager at Eli Lilly and Company in Indianapolis, working for Xerox Business Services. We managed a large print shop for Eli Lilly and were working on a large project that had to get submitted to the Food and Drug Administration (FDA) for approval. If it didn't get submitted on time, it had time-to-market implications for Eli Lilly that could be in the millions of dollars in lost revenue. As if our focus needed to be sharpened any more, I promised our team if we completed the project on time, we'd go to Kings Island amusement park for the day as a thank you. We were a bunch of young adults at the time, and while a relatively small reward, I remember being surprised at how much our team appreciated this.

- **Communicate the vision.** It is critically important in a team setting for people to understand what we're trying to accomplish. A team without goals and direction is much like a ship without a rudder. Additionally, a strong team vision should get people excited. Honest, hard-working people like to work on big things and be a part of big ideas. Donald Trump, a billionaire businessman and our current President, once said, "If you are going to be thinking anyway, think big."

To illustrate, I was leading an operations team for Xerox in 1995, and at the beginning of the year, we spent a good amount of time developing a Mission Statement for our team. At a quarterly recognition meeting, I happened to mention to another manager that my entire team had bought into our Mission Statement and knew it by heart. He was skeptical, so I challenged him to ask anybody on my team what our Mission Statement was. We had spent quite a bit of time developing it as a group, so I was highly confident anyone he asked would be able to recite it, word for word. He asked the first person on our team that he saw, who proceeded to stumble over it badly. I was surprised and disappointed, as we had spent a lot of time on this. So, the next week I started calling my team and asking them to recite it to me over the phone (my team worked in various client locations). Word traveled quickly regarding my phone calls. I remember one team member, Barb Stevens, joking with me, "Mike, you must not have enough to do if you have time to call all of us and ask us to recite our Mission Statement." Without hesitation, I responded, "Barb, there is nothing I could be doing with my time that is more important than to ensure everyone on our team understands what we are trying to accomplish."

(5) Make People Feel a Part of Something Special

Another characteristic of a leader is they make you feel like you are a part of something bigger than yourself. One way this can be done is to help people understand how what they do fits into a larger picture. Leaders make sure people know not only what the overall direction of the organization is, but what their individual role is inside that direction.

In a family setting, an example might be making sure kids understand they are representing the entire family when they go to school or church. If they lie or are not kind to others, that reflects negatively on the entire family. I was recently watching a biography on TV about Pete Rose on ESPN Classic. For those of you who don't know, Pete Rose is the all-time hits leader in Major League Baseball, accumulating 4,256 hits over a 24-year career. Rose was known as "Charlie Hustle," largely based on how hard he played. When asked about his legendary work ethic, Rose recalled a minor league game in which he hit a lazy fly ball to the outfield that resulted in a routine out. The young Rose had jogged to first base. His dad was at the game and afterward told Pete, "When you're on the ball field, you are not just representing yourself, but you're representing me also. I just wanted to call your attention to the fact you didn't run all out to first base on that fly ball in the 5th inning." He didn't yell at him, didn't dwell on it, but Rose's dad made his point. From that game on, Pete Rose sprinted to first base, be it a walk, fly ball, or a hit. "Charlie Hustle" was born on that day, in part because his dad exhibited leadership.

I had a personal experience with this while running an operations team back in the 1995/1996 time frame while at Xerox. We had a team whose sole purpose was to provide backup for employees who worked on site at customer locations. Xerox had outsourcing contracts whereby we ran print shops and managed copier fleets on a customer's location. Our contracts included backup services for personnel in the event someone was on vacation or called in sick.

Upon picking up responsibility for this team, we took this a step further. We began to view ourselves as internal consultants and began providing training in addition to backup services to our employees to further the service we as a company were providing to our customers. One way we did this was we recruited the "best of the best" internally and sold them on the vision of what we were trying to accomplish as a team. Back in those days, Xerox tracked customer satisfaction very closely. We believed by putting our best people in backup roles, and training the very people we were backing up on equipment, customer satisfaction skills, productivity, and output quality, we could move the needle for the entire organization's customer satisfaction scores. We, in fact, did. During our monthly team meetings, we would review our own satisfaction scores against some very aggressive goals we set for ourselves, and during this time our division saw some of the highest customer satisfaction scores we'd ever seen.

Perhaps the greatest compliment I've ever received as a leader came from one of my employees during this time frame. We had recruited her to join our team because she was a very good production operator. I remember asking her about six months after she joined our team how things were going. She said she really liked it, and that one reason she did is that I made her and the team feel like what they did was important and that they were making a difference. The truth is she and our team were making a difference. Our division's customer satisfaction scores proved it. I truly believed our team could "move the needle" on our entire division's customer satisfaction scores. And because I believed it with such great conviction, they believed it too. We kept score publicly, recognized people's contributions regularly, and reminded them constantly of what we were trying to accomplish. In short, we had total buy-in.

A byproduct of getting our team feeling like they were a part of something special came in the area of recruiting. Being a part of the backup team was not something anyone wanted to do prior to me picking up responsibility for the team. There were some downsides to this job. For example, you were sometimes called at the last minute to go somewhere else. We had some accounts that worked shift work (meaning after hours or in the middle of the night), so the workweek was often a nonstandard workweek. That said, word traveled fast that we were a team on the move and with a mission. When we added headcount, we would put up internal job postings. Prior to my arrival, we had to beg people to join this team. Afterward, we had multiple people respond to job postings, and in some cases, we had to turn good people away. What was the difference? People yearn to be a part of something special, even if it requires more effort and more flexibility on their part. And make no mistake, people like being part of a winning team.

(6) Influence Others

In a nutshell, leadership is mostly about influence. If you don't have influence over others, then nobody will follow you. Colin Powell once said, "You have achieved excellence as a leader when people will follow you everywhere if only out of curiosity." I came across a leadership proverb that went like this: *He who thinks he leads but has no followers is merely taking a walk.*

Leadership does not automatically come with a title and responsibility. It can't be assigned, awarded, or dictated. It has to be earned, and sometimes earned over time. Having a title is nice, but that title only buys you a little time. It does not buy you leadership or influence. A great example of this comes from the Royal Family in Great Britain. In 1981, Prince Charles of England married Lady Diana Frances Spencer. Although the daughter of an earl, the new Princess Diana had led an ordinary life and was, at one point, a kindergarten teacher. The world certainly knew who Prince Charles was, but no one knew much about Princess Diana. She was at first very shy and seemed a bit overwhelmed with the attention she was receiving. Over time, she grew into her role, focusing her time and attention on various charities. She also spent a great deal of time bringing attention to the AIDS disease and helping raise money for research.

Sadly, the couple divorced in 1996. But that did not diminish her role. Interestingly, post-divorce Princess Diana continued to be known as a Princess, more famous than her ex-husband Prince Charles. Prince Charles had the royal title and position, but Princess Diana wielded far more influence over world events than Prince Charles ever did.

(7) Build Trust

There can be no leadership without trust. Trust comes chiefly from doing three things.

First, leaders never lie to their people. Once you've lied to someone, in any setting, at any time, they will never trust you again. Period. And if you're a dad and you lie to your kids, what are you teaching them?

Secondly, leaders communicate to people what is going on. When your team is left in the dark, it is human nature to assume the worst. Conversely, when you are keeping people informed, they feel a part of things. I had a situation when I was an Operations Manager at Xerox around 1996. There was a young man on my team (we will call him James) that had a medical issue that periodically caused him to have seizures. In fact, he had two seizures while at work, where we had to call an ambulance for him. He was a young man that we had some productivity issues with independent of his medical issue, and he had attendance issues also. My heart went out to him, but we just didn't have a role where he could be productive for us. We tried moving him around at the suggestion of one of my supervisors, but we just couldn't find a fit for him.

I came to the conclusion over a period of months that we needed to let this young man go. This wasn't an easy decision, but it was the right one. I knew this may not be a popular decision, as I noticed we had a few people who felt sorry for him and had formed the habit of trying to help him and cover up for him. But when you're a leader, sometimes tough calls need to be made.

I feared people would think his seizures were the cause of his dismissal, which was not the case. So, the same day we let him go, I called the entire team together to tell them what decision had been made, but more importantly why. While everyone knew James had attendance issues, I explained to them that I never counted the time he missed work due to having a seizure against him. Also, I was able to compare his productivity while healthy to that of the rest of the team. I then asked them who are we being fair to by keeping someone on our team who doesn't measure up to the goals we've set for ourselves? Is it fair to you, the rest of the team, to have two different sets of standards—one for James and one for the rest of you? Framed this way, it got the very people whose support I needed thinking about the issue differently. Instead of the issue being about what is best for James, we made it about what is best and fair for the entire team. This changed the entire conversation. There is no 'I' in TEAM, so as we make decisions it must be about what is best for the entire team. Now we had total buy-in, not just on this issue, but on every issue that came up thereafter.

We continued to ask ourselves questions. Is it fair to our clients? Is it fair to our company to keep someone on the payroll who is not pulling their own weight? Is it fair to our shareholders? And finally, are we really being fair to James by allowing a minor disability to be an excuse for poor performance? Long term, I would say no. This may seem harsh, but I don't think it is. When people have a disability, you absolutely have to make accommodations for them, as it is the right and fair thing to do. But, those accommodations should be reasonable. In my view, a reasonable accommodation does not mean you have two completely different sets of standards.

And one final question I posed to our team: if we establish that we will make exceptions for people, then where do those exceptions stop? While I know a few people disagreed with my decision, they at least understood where I was coming from. And because I took the time to explain my decision and demonstrated to them it was well thought out, I think they trusted me even more despite the fact some disagreed with me. Finally, a side benefit to getting the entire team together was we discussed the situation as a group, cleared the air a bit, and eliminated the rumor mill, as everyone heard the same message at the same time. This could have been an issue that fractured and distracted our team. Instead, I think it ultimately brought us closer together.

Third, leaders are consistent. You can't lead a group of people, or a family, if you make haphazard decisions, and if your focus is all over the map. Another component of being consistent is you have to treat people similarly in similar situations. Now, I didn't say treat everyone the same. People are different with different interests, and so what motivates one person might not work for another. My two older kids, a 14-year-old son and 11-year-old daughter, are very different. I sometimes have to be hard (and loud) with my 14-year-old son to get his attention, yet my 11-year-old will start crying if I simply give her a dirty look. While they are held accountable to the same standards, be it homework or cleaning their rooms, how I go about it is very different because they are very different people.

While you don't treat people the same, it is very important you are consistent in similar situations. Let's take a business setting. Let's say you have one employee who is often late, so you give him a written warning after five occurrences. Yet for another employee who shows up for work late, you only provide two warnings prior to a written notice. This would be an example of being inconsistent. Nothing breaks down a leader's credibility and trust with their people more than inconsistency.

(8) Recognize Accomplishments

Leaders go out of their way to recognize the behaviors that they want to see. This is what I like to call a "twofer." First, it makes the person you're recognizing feel better about themselves, and it lets them know you appreciate what they are doing. This makes it more likely they will continue to do what you need them to do. Second, it also reinforces to the entire team what you are looking for. Recognizing accomplishments publicly is an easy yet highly effective way to build morale for the entire organization (or, in this case, a family). "Win their hearts, and their minds will follow" is a leadership mantra that almost always works. Recognizing accomplishments and going out of your way to show people you appreciate them goes a long way to "winning their hearts."

Below are a few examples where I've seen recognition and going out of your way to show appreciation pay dividends.

I've spent a good chunk of my career in a sales role. As such, I need access to executive-level decision makers from time to time to review proposals and ideas. In today's world of 24/7 cable news, social media, email, voice mail, satellite radio, and texting, it can be difficult to get an executive's attention. One thing I've done to address this is to find out who their executive assistant is, and to treat them with the same level of respect I would as if I'm talking to the executive. When it comes to getting a meeting, the assistant is the executive. To show my appreciation, I'll buy a Starbucks gift card for the assistants I work with around the holidays to show them I appreciate their help in scheduling meetings. Showing them both respect and appreciation has been very helpful for me over the years in getting meetings when I need them. Put another way, who do you think an assistant is more likely to help—a person who is rude, short, and condescending over the phone, or a person who is respectful, patient, and thanks them with a periodic gift card?

Another example comes early in my career while I was working for Xerox Business Services. I worked for a true leader, George Hodgson, who was the General Manager over a three-state operation. He used to have Quarterly Recognition Meetings, where we got the entire team together to review the state of the business and to provide awards for the top performers. These meetings were typically held over dinner and could get quite expensive. However, in retrospect, I think they were worth every penny. I thought reviewing the business with the entire team was extremely valuable, in that it kept people informed and engaged in the business overall. Regarding the recognition portion, this included all departments—Sales, Operations, and Administration. Thus, recognition was very public, cross-departmental, and was a great way to build morale, especially for the people that were fulfilling roles that were important, but not high profile.

(9) Hold People Accountable

People (adults and kids alike) tend to rise to the level that is expected of them. That said, nothing breaks down a team faster than when laziness or subpar performance is not confronted. If poor performance is tolerated, then one of a couple of things will happen. First, your top performers will leave, as they don't want to be around poor performers. Second, above-average performers that stay will start to lower their standards, as below average to low performance takes less effort. Either way, the entire team's performance begins to decline—a direct reflection on the leader.

Early in my career, I had a college buddy living with me. By this point, I had won several awards as an Operations Manager for superior performance, and as a result, had brought home several plaques. After about the third one I brought home, he asked me what my secret was. This was an insightful question, one I had not given much thought to up to that point. After thinking about it for a minute, I came up with the following:

- Those that get the job done, I praise the heck out of them publicly.

- Those that don't get the job done, I get rid of them.

To this day, I have found this formula to be highly effective, yet incredibly simple. By rewarding what you are looking for, publicly, you remind and reinforce the behaviors you are looking for to the entire team. This approach is also highly effective with kids. Rather than yell at my son for not making his bed or cleaning his room, I will reward his sister for doing these things right in front of him, and before long, he is back on track because he wants to be rewarded too.

Regarding poor performers, you certainly need to give people a chance to improve their performance. Most people want to do a good job; they just need additional guidance if they are falling short of expectations. That said, if you've provided clear direction and have given a person multiple opportunities to bring their performance up to expectations, and they are still falling short, then they have to go. Only the leader can do this. And by removing poor performers, you build loyalty with your top performers and eliminate the distraction of those that aren't pulling their own weight.

My first job with Xerox was the role of Production Supervisor. I inherited a team that was not very good. Six months after my arrival, we were even worse. We had one individual, we'll call him Ralph, who was by far our worst performer. He single-handedly represented 30 percent of our quality issues on a 12-person team. I finally let him go, as it was obvious his performance, despite multiple chances and multiple written warnings, was not improving. A surprising thing happened after this incident. My better performers rallied behind me, as I was one of the first supervisors that had addressed his poor performance in such a decisive way. Morale for the entire team improved, and we ultimately catapulted our way from last in our division to second out of eight teams. This taught me a valuable lesson. Good performers want people to be held accountable for their performance. The good ones will improve and rise up, and those that don't must go.

Being a Father

As I thought through the preceding nine leadership qualities, I quickly realized what a true leader my own father was. To this day, I still turn to him for advice and counsel when faced with difficult decisions or challenging situations. I also realized that if I turn out to be half the father to my kids that my dad was to me, I'll be in pretty good shape. And far more important, so will my kids.

Thank you, Dad! The footprints are there to follow.

The passage below was a late but valuable addition to the book. It came from a mom named Sarah Driscoll, who has a blog called *Diapers and Daisies*. Sarah has a web site you might want to check out (www.sarahdriscoll.com). As I've had a chance to read a few of her blogs, she has a very common-sense approach to life in general. This particular passage was posted many years ago. Given the theme of this book, I thought it hit the nail on the head.

28 Rules for Fathers and Sons

1. Love his Mother.

He will learn to love like you love, and hate like you hate. So choose love for both of you. Devote yourself to it. Love with your whole heart and express that love each and every day. Then, someday down the road, you will see the way he loves his own wife, and know that you played a part in that.

2. Let him drive.

Every child remembers the first time they drove on Daddy's lap. For that one moment, he will believe that he is just like you.

3. Teach him to be picky.

Especially when it comes to women and burgers. Teach him to never settle.

4. Take him to a ball game.

There is something about sharing a day of hot dogs, sunshine, and baseball with your Father.

5. Love with bravery.

Boys have this preconceived notion that they have to be tough. When he is young, he will express his love fully and innocently. As he grows, he will hide his feelings and wipe off kisses. Teach him to be a man who rubs them in instead. It takes courage for a man to show love: teach him to be courageous.

6. Talk about sex.

Sometimes, boys need to know that all men are created equal.

7. Teach him to be a man's man.

Show him how to be brave and tough around the guys. Then, remind him on the ride home that it is okay to cry.

8. Share secrets together.

Communicate. Talk. Talk about anything. Let him tell you about girls, friends, school. Listen. Ask questions. Share dreams, hopes, concerns. He is not only your son; you are not only his father. Be his friend too.

9. Teach him manners.

Because sometimes you have to be his Father, not just his friend. The world is a happier place when made up of polite words and smiles.

10. Teach him when to stand up and when to walk away.

He should know that he doesn't have to throw punches to prove he is right. He may not always be right. Make sure he knows how to demand respect—he is worthy of it. It does not mean he has to fight back with fists or words, because sometimes you say more with silence.

11. Teach him to choose his battles.

Make sure he knows which battles are worth fighting—like for family or his favorite baseball team. Remind him that people can be mean and nasty because of jealousy, or other personal reasons. Help him to understand when to shut his mouth and walk away. Teach him to be the better person.

12. Let him dance in tighty whiteys.

Dance alongside him in yours. Teach him that there are moments when it is okay to be absolutely ridiculous.

13. Share music.

Introduce him to the classics and learn the words to the not-so-classics. Create a rock band with wooden instruments, share your earphones, and blast Pink Floyd in the car. Create a soundtrack to your lives together.

14. Let him win.

Sometimes he needs to know that big things are possible.

15. Teach him about family.

Let him know family is always worth fighting for. Family is always worth standing up for. At the end of the day, he has you to fall back on, and pray to God that you will have him.

16. Father him.

Being a father to him is undoubtedly one of your greatest accomplishments. Share with him the joys of fatherhood, so one day he will want to be a Father too. Remind him over and over again with words and kisses that no one will ever love him like you love him.

17. Listen to him now.

If you don't listen to the little things now, he won't share the big things later.

18. Let him try on your shoes.

Even if they are old and smelly. Let him slip his little feet in and watch him as he hopes like hell that someday he can fill them. He will fill them.

19. Give him bear hugs.

The kind that squeezes his insides and makes him giggle. The kind of hug only a daddy can give.

20. Give him baths.

Because Mom can't do everything.

21. Teach him how to pee standing up.

Let him pee outside—such is the joy of being a man. Mom cannot teach this talent, so someone has to.

22. Know the answers.

He will assume you do. If you don't know them, pretend you do and look them up later.

A Collection of Thoughts

23. Toss him around.

Because little boys love seeing the strength of their Father. Throw him up in the air, so that he knows you will always be there to catch him on his way down.

24. Ask his Mother.

He will come to you with questions that he won't always want to ask his Mother, about girls and about love. Ask her anyway, she will know the answers.

25. Love him like you would love a daughter.

Little girls are not the only ones who need hugs and kisses. Love is the color yellow of emotions. It is both happy and gender neutral.

26. Grow a big belly.

Because every child should get the chance to rest their head on the absolute softest pillow ever. Daddy's belly is the best place to land.

27. Don't say, do.

American inventor Charles F. Kettering once said, "Every Father should remember that one day his son will follow his example instead of his advice." Be a good one.

28. Be his hero.

You are anyway. To him, you have the strength of Batman, the speed of Spiderman, and the brain of Ironman. Don't disappoint him. Prove to him that Daddys are the biggest heroes of all. Only Daddys can save the day.

CHAPTER

PERSONAL VALUES
WHAT'S YOUR COMPASS?

What is a value? According to *Webster's New World Dictionary*, a few nonmonetary definitions include (1) that quality of a thing which makes it more or less desirable or useful, (2) a thing or quality having intrinsic worth, (3) beliefs or standards.

What's Your Compass?

To put this into parental terms, I think values are belief systems you not only pass on to your kids, but you also hope those belief systems become a roadmap for your children throughout their lives. A value system should help them make decisions as they repeatedly come to the proverbial fork in the road. When kids and young adults have to decide between what is right and what is popular—which are not always one and the same—what will help guide and influence those decisions when you as a parent aren't around to help them? Children have to make all kinds of decisions as they grow. Should I do my homework or watch TV? Should I participate in making fun of one of my classmates because everyone else is, or should I not participate and stick up for the kid that might be a little different? Should I experiment with drugs because it's popular, or will I have the fortitude to "just say no" and risk being made fun of myself?

Values become a set of standards to judge right from wrong, good from bad, and hopefully enable your children to make good decisions that are based on fairness, kindness, good judgment, and common sense.

A Collection of Thoughts

As I thought through what values were important to pass along to my own children, I once again didn't have to look far for the blueprint. I simply reviewed how my mom and dad raised my sister and me and applied that experience to my own thinking.

Therefore, we will discuss four key values:

- Honesty
- Loyalty
- Character
- Integrity

Honesty

My own father had a couple of sayings as it related to honesty. One is a cliché: "Honesty is the best policy." The other was one I think he came up with on his own: "If you always tell the truth, then you won't have to worry about remembering what you said."

When I made mistakes, as all kids do, my dad was good about not only correcting me but also making sure there was a lesson to be learned. One such example came when I was about eleven or twelve years old. I was doing some odd jobs around the neighborhood to make a little money. The jobs included cutting grass, pulling weeds, trimming bushes, and feeding pets while the owners were away.

I happened to get one job that entailed removing weeds from a small sand embankment, or small beach. The owner lived on a small lake and had weeds growing all over his beach. My job was to remove all the weeds, which proved to be a far more laborious task than I had realized. The job was extremely tedious. After working for about two hours, I probably completed about half the job and grew bored with the task. So, rather than complete the job I was being paid for, I took a rake and raked the sand over the remaining weeds that had not been removed so they would not show. Feeling pretty good about my own ingenuity, I returned home after just a couple of hours.

As I rode my bike up our driveway, my dad was in the garage and seemed a bit surprised I was home already. The ensuing conversation went something like this:

Dad: "Are you done already?"
Me: "Yes."

Dad: "You finished the job you were paid to do?"
Me: "Yes."

Dad: "You pulled every weed out of that beach!?" (He was starting to get loud.)
Me: "Well, most of them." (I was already quite the conversationalist even at an early age.)

Dad: "What does most of them mean?" (My dad was fully aware of how many weeds were in this sandy lakeside beach. He surmised, correctly, I'm afraid, that had I done a thorough job I would not be home yet.)
Me: "I pulled about half of them and raked the sand over the other half." Quite proudly, I proclaimed: "You can't see a single weed on the beach!"

Dad: "So you're telling me you were paid to do a job, and you only completed 50 percent of it?"
Me: "Well, you can't see any weeds, which is what he was paying me to do." (I wasn't sure where this conversation was going and didn't want to stick around to find out, so I started to head for the door to the house.)

Dad: "Hold it. Hold it! If someone pays you to do a job, then you're going to finish it. You were paid to remove weeds, not hide them. When does Mr. Johnson (fictitious name) get home?"
Me: "Tomorrow afternoon, I think."

Dad: "What do you think you should do?"
Me: "Well, I guess I should go back over there to finish the job before he gets home."

Feeling quite satisfied even my dad would agree this was the right thing to do, I started to head for my bike, reluctantly I might add, to head back over and complete the job. My dad was always opportunistic when it came to teaching me a life lesson and wasn't about to let this one go.

Dad: "Hold it! Mike, this isn't about how many weeds you pulled. The reason I'm making a big deal about this is a man that can't be trusted in small matters will never be trusted in large matters. Mr. Johnson trusted you to do a job, and you betrayed that trust

A Collection of Thoughts

by not finishing the job. The easy thing to do would be to finish it after you had already made a decision not to finish it. That's a dishonest approach that is also taking the easy way out. No son of mine will take either path."

Me: "What am I supposed to do?"

Dad: "When Mr. Johnson gets home tomorrow afternoon, I want you to give him half his money back."

Me: "What!? Why?" I asked.

Dad: "Because you only finished half the job!" (By this time he was a little irritated with me and wasn't looking for my opinion.)

Giving Mr. Johnson half his money back didn't seem to be a particularly good idea to me. After all, I had worked for two hours, and you couldn't see any weeds at the moment—the task he was ultimately paying me to do. I also agreed I would go back over there to finish the job before Mr. Johnson returned home. "What am I supposed to say?" I asked.

As my dad looked right through me, a look I, unfortunately, saw from time to time growing up, he said, "Just tell him the truth, Mike. Just tell him the truth." Life would be much simpler if everyone followed this simple value.

To make a long story short, I rode my bike over to Mr. Johnson's house the next day. With all the courage I had, I rang the doorbell. As he opened the door, my chest was pounding, my palms were sweaty, and I was a bit scared. However, the fear of telling my neighbor what I had done was not nearly as great as the fear of telling my dad I had not only not done what he had instructed me to do, but that I had also chickened out as well.

I proceeded to tell Mr. Johnson what I had done and offered to give him half of his money back. When I was finished, he thanked me for telling him the truth. "It took a lot of courage for you to come over here and tell me that." To my surprise, he didn't seem mad. "That sort of honesty and courage should be rewarded with a second chance," he said. He told me if I wanted to finish the job that day, I could keep the money he had paid me—in full. With my dad's words ringing in my ears, "finish what you start," I immediately agreed to finish the job.

It took me about another two hours to thoroughly complete the job. As I rode my bike home, exhausted, a feeling of pride came over me that I'm not sure I had felt before up to that point in my life. I felt good about the fact I had finished what I had started. I felt good about the fact I had summoned up the courage to tell the truth, even though it would have been far easier to have avoided the conversation with Mr. Johnson entirely. I felt good about the fact I could tell my dad I had done exactly what he had told me to do. And, oh yes, I was proud that I was able to keep 100 percent of the money. As I pedaled home, I couldn't wait to tell my dad how this had turned out.

My dad had a knack for tying multiple lessons into a single situation. When I got home and told him what had transpired, he was pleased. Upon completing my story, my dad asked me a question I would hear from time to time as I got older: "What did you learn?"

Another quick story regarding honesty involves fast-forwarding to my senior year of high school. I grew up in a small town, Brownsburg, Indiana. During homecoming week, each class at Brownsburg High School would build a float for our annual homecoming parade. It was an unwritten tradition that the different classes would try to tamper with, or egg, another class's float. Thus, a few of my buddies and I went out looking for under-classman floats and were going to egg them. I know this was a juvenile, dopey thing to do, but we were dumb kids at the time. At any rate, we were driving slowly through a neighborhood looking for a float party; and getting suspicious, someone that lived there followed us. Once we realized we were being followed, we quickly left. I happened to be driving, and upon getting home, my dad was waiting for me. He asked me what I had been doing, and I told him, conveniently leaving out the part about our plans to egg a homecoming float.

He asked me very sternly, "Do you want to try again?" Seeing he was mad, I said, "No, I don't think so." I wasn't sure what was going on and thought the less I said, the better. He proceeded to tell me the police had called him, as the neighbor that had followed me wrote down my license plate number and called the police. Apparently, someone had egged his truck that was sitting in his driveway. We didn't do it, but we were in the area and certainly looked suspicious, driving slowly through the neighborhood. We would have easily been convicted on circumstantial evidence, as we were near the scene of the vandalism, and did, in fact, have eggs in the car.

Upon hearing the whole story, and seeing the carton of eggs in the car was still full, my dad believed me. He believed me because over the years I had always told the truth. I was certainly not a perfect kid growing up, but I did tell the truth. My parents always told me if I do something I'm not supposed to, I'll get in far more trouble if I lie about it, and get into less trouble if I simply told them the truth. That said, my dad did make me go down to the police station and explain the situation to the Chief of Police, not a real comfortable thing to do for an 18-year-old kid. Even in doing the right thing, my dad couldn't resist reinforcing a lesson.

Life Lessons

- Finish what you start.
- Things are always simpler if you tell the truth—in the short and long run.
- If you always tell the truth, you don't have to remember what you said.
- Take pride in what you do.

Loyalty

Growing up, it became obvious to me my dad was pretty good at what he did. I guess many sons look up to their fathers and see them as outstanding at their trade. In my case, I think this opinion was justified. My dad was an Operations Manager and developed a reputation for being firm but fair with subordinates. He began his career as a Supervisor, moved up the ranks to a Manager, Director, and then Vice President of a mortgage company, and later retired as a President of a small mail operation. Obviously, if you continue to expand your levels of responsibility as your career unfolds, you must be doing a lot of things right.

As my dad moved along in his career, he was offered a number of promotions that would require relocating his family. As best I can recall, he was offered a position in Stamford, Connecticut; Chicago; and San Diego to name a few. I think he was offered about four positions in a ten-year period, precisely the time frame when my sister and I were at a formative age.

While I remember him seriously considering at least one of those positions, in Chicago I think, he ultimately turned all of them down. I can still remember, at times, with some anxiety over potentially having to move and make new friends, our family discussing the pros and cons of such a move. As you can imagine, my mom and dad were doing most of the talking. However, the sole reason for turning down career advancement opportunities always came down to one simple question, "What was best for the entire family?" Not what was best for my dad, or my dad's career, but what was best for his kids.

My sister Karen and I always knew we were loved, and always knew we came first to my dad (my mom too, but that is for another book). We knew it not so much because of what he said, but by watching his actions. I mentioned the link between leadership and fatherhood in the opening chapter. Sometimes leaders can make a strong statement without actually saying anything. Turning down career advancement opportunities because it wasn't in the best interest of his kids spoke volumes. What did my sister and I learn? True love is when you're willing to put someone else's needs before your own. We learned this lesson without my mom or dad uttering a single word. Priceless.

As I have gotten into the prime of my own career, I've known many people who moved their families all over the country, regardless of what age their children were, and regardless of what kind of impact it had on them. While there is nothing wrong with taking career advancement opportunities that require relocation, parents should take into account what kind of impact such a move will have on their family. Timing is also a key consideration. Moving kids away from their friends at a young age may not be that big of a deal. Relocating kids at the Junior High or High School age can be traumatic on a child who has close friends.

I saw this firsthand. We did, in fact, make one move while I was growing up out of necessity. My dad was working for a company that was struggling financially and was in the midst of laying off employees due to cutbacks. Fortunately, my dad was not around long enough to get his pink slip. We relocated when I was in the fifth grade, and my sister was in eighth grade. Being younger and a boy, the move was not a huge ordeal for me. The first few days were a little scary. The first few weeks were awkward, and I felt a little out of place. However, within a couple of months, I felt right at home. My sister, being in the eighth grade, I think, found it more difficult to make new friends. She ultimately did, but the transition was not nearly as smooth or as quick for her.

I still remember the feeling of relief (as if it were yesterday) every time my dad would turn down an opportunity for advancement. I also remember committing to myself that my family and children would come before my own career when I was old enough to be put in the same position.

Some people talk about how their family comes first, and in many cases, they are being sincere when they say it. Only a few men truly make decisions that are consistent with what they say when it comes to balancing careers and family life. As far as my dad was concerned, "loyalty to family first" wasn't a good conversational piece at a cocktail party—he lived it consistently. There is an old Irish saying that captures this topic perfectly: "Loyalty above all else, but Honor."

One final story I received from Bob Proctor, a notable author, motivational speaker, and teacher, depicts loyalty to the extreme. The story by Rick Reilly for *Sports Illustrated* tells how one father put his son first.

Life Lessons

- Be loyal to your family—first and always.

- To receive loyalty, you must first be loyal.

- True love is when you are willing to put another person's needs before your own.

Character

I was a pretty good all-around athlete growing up. I played football, basketball, and baseball from the age of seven through my high school years. I also managed to get in some golf and tennis, although I never played either sport in an organized fashion. I was a pretty decent quarterback in football, owning a career record of 19-3 as a starter as an eighth-grader, freshman, and sophomore in high school. That said, I knew "pretty decent" wasn't good enough. There was a kid who was a year ahead of me in school. Simply put, he was a better quarterback than I was. I wouldn't have gotten a chance to play varsity football until my senior year.

For those of you who have played football at the high school level, you know how much work is involved in playing football. There is mandatory conditioning during the summer, required weight lifting, and two-a-day practices in August. I decided, for me, that was too much work given I wouldn't get a chance to play until I was a senior. That, and given my true love was basketball, I decided before my junior year to give up football so I could focus on basketball and baseball.

There are several reasons why basketball had been my favorite sport.

First, I grew up in Indiana in the 1970s and 1980s. As a result, I was a huge Bob Knight fan. (Bob Knight was head coach of Indiana University's basketball team from 1971 to 2000.) I practically learned to count watching

Indiana basketball games on television. I used to keep the stats on my own sheet of paper while I watched the games with my dad. I can still remember watching Kent Benson hit a hook shot over a Michigan defender to seal the NCAA championship for Indiana in 1976, which incidentally capped an undefeated season.

Second, my dad played collegiate basketball, having earned a full-ride scholarship to play for Tony Hinkle's Butler Bulldogs in 1961. As a result, my dad had forgotten more about the game of basketball than most people know. Thus, I think my love affair with the game of basketball was preordained.

Third, basketball was, in my opinion, a perfect balance of skill, athletic ability, and stamina. I thought it was the best game ever invented.

The high school coach at Brownsburg was a guy named Doug Huse. I had the opportunity to play for Coach Huse during a summer league between my seventh-grade and eighth-grade years. He was a fiery guy who knew a lot about the game of basketball. In fact, he reminded me a lot of my dad. Coach Huse decided to leave coaching and teaching to pursue a more financially lucrative career selling insurance, so he resigned shortly before my eighth-grade year ended. I was crushed. Coach Huse had already told my dad I would be playing on the junior varsity team as a freshman. I thought if I worked hard, I had a chance to be a three-year starter on the varsity team—not many people achieve that in a larger school system like Brownsburg High School.

Specific to basketball, I had set three goals for myself. First, I would lead Brownsburg to the Final Four of Indiana's High School Basketball tournament. Second, I would make the Indiana All-Star team as a senior, a team that plays Kentucky's High School All-Stars in a home and away series every year. Third, I would play college basketball for none other than Coach Bob Knight at Indiana University.

The day I learned Coach Huse, the Bob Knight of High School basketball, in my opinion, had resigned, I was simply crushed. My love of the game ended; I drifted, I stopped working as hard; I wasn't as passionate about the game as I had been. In a word, I became complacent (more on that later).

His replacement was a former assistant coach who had never played the game before. Now, I don't care how well-intentioned you are, it is exceedingly difficult to be able to coach and teach a game, or anything for that matter, that you have never played or participated in.

I tried to go into this new situation with an open mind, but my worst fears were quickly realized. Coach Huse's replacement, while a nice man, was not as knowledgeable, was not a leader, was not a disciplinarian. And also, as it turned out, was not as big of a "Mike Johns fan" as Coach Huse was. That said, the real issue wasn't the new coach; it was me. As a result of my not working as hard, several other kids had closed the skills gap on me. With my passion for the game burning like a boy scout fire in the rain, I was not the same player. While I did ultimately play varsity basketball for three years, I was nothing more than a role player, having never started a single game my entire career. My dream of being a three-year starter had evaporated.

My basketball career was a shadow of what I dreamed it would be; what it should have been. There were many games and countless practices when I would drive home afterward, completely dejected with how things were going. In my senior year, our team was a mediocre basketball team with a losing record. In all the years I played basketball, I had never been a part of a losing team. Individually I was a limited role player. Because our team was mediocre, my limited contributions were that much more difficult to swallow. Having been a starter and the leading scorer on every team I played on from fourth grade up to my sophomore year in high school (seven years in a row), I now played sparingly on a team that wasn't very good. This was a hard, bitter pill to swallow. This was my first taste of failure, failure at achieving something I had set out to do. However, despite an extreme amount of frustration and disappointment, I never publicly complained and didn't quit.

At the conclusion of the basketball season my senior year, I received a call from the local editor of *The Guide* asking me to come down to his office. *The Guide* was a local newspaper for the town of Brownsburg, which is located on the northwest side of Indianapolis. At that time, *The Guide* probably had a circulation of around 25,000. We ended up getting together on a Saturday morning in late March 1987. I was intrigued as to why the editor of *The Guide* wanted me to come down to his office. I wasn't the star of the team, wasn't involved in any trouble or controversies, certainly wasn't running for public office, and was perplexed as to why he wanted to see me. As far as I knew, he had no idea who I was. I agreed to drive down to his office more out of curiosity than anything else.

When I walked into his office, the editor introduced himself. After a few minutes of pleasantries, he presented me with a plaque with an engraving. I quickly found myself overwhelmed with emotion. The engraving read as follows:

MIKE JOHNS

In Appreciation For
His Perseverance And
Dedication To Brownsburg
High School Basketball.

This Award Is
Presented By Grateful
Basketball Fans.

March 1987

I was speechless. I was also extraordinarily grateful. It took me a few minutes to gather myself. Once I had collected my thoughts, I asked the editor who was responsible for presenting this to me. I was told by the editor it wasn't one person, but an outpouring of people that chipped in to give me that plaque. He never gave me a single name. I wanted to thank the people who did that for me, as it meant a lot to me. It was a real shot in the arm at a time when I really needed it. That was a difficult time for me, but I'll always regret not knowing who all was responsible for the award, as I would have liked to have had the opportunity to thank them; thank every last one of them. While I think I've lost or misplaced many of my trophies from my childhood, that plaque is something I still have to this day. I keep it in my home office and look at it periodically as a reminder of how much perseverance and a positive attitude is appreciated.

Valuable Lessons

While the experience of playing high school basketball was disappointing, it did teach me a few valuable lessons that have served me well during my professional career.

First, don't ever become complacent.

Natural ability will only take you so far, regardless of how much talent you think you have. You still need to have a plan for success and work that plan. An attitude and approach of seeking continuous improvement and building plans to get better at what you do professionally will ensure that you never become complacent. Why? Because you will be constantly seeking ways to raise the bar on your performance. You don't become complacent when you are stretching your own ceiling, when you are continuously competing against yourself. Don't strive to be the smart kid in the dumb row. Strive to be the best you can be, and then set about continually trying to be better than your previous self.

To build on this first lesson, a good practice to get into if you want to be successful in your chosen field, is to set high expectations for yourself. If you expect and demand more from yourself than anyone above you does, then you will never have to worry about job security. When times are lean, companies tend to cut payrolls in an attempt to cut expenses. Managers will stack rank employees during this process. Guess which ones are let go first? You guessed it. The ones stack ranked toward the bottom. Regarding expectations, I'll give you two examples.

Example 1: I mentioned Coach Knight and his undefeated National Championship team in 1976 in an earlier section. What I didn't mention is his 1975 team entered the NCAA tournament undefeated also (31-0). They were defeated in the Elite 8 by Kentucky 92-90, largely due to an injury to their leading scorer Scott May. At the beginning of the 1975-1976 season, Coach Knight told his team, which had many returning starters, what he expected—an undefeated season. Based on a clear goal and high expectations, his team delivered, going 32-0 and winning the National Championship.

Example 2: Think back to your childhood, and think of who your most demanding teacher was growing up. Now, think of which teacher was your favorite. Invariably these two are one and the same. Demanding teachers force you to stretch by maintaining high expectations, and through high expectations, we tend to learn more, and therefore, achieve more. A demanding teacher who shows an interest in you is a gift. My two all-time favorite teachers, and two first ballot hall-of-famers in my book, are as follows:

• Mrs. DelaGarza was my sixth-grade teacher. She had a reading contest throughout the year, where we tracked who read the most books. As I look back on it, she inspired me to get in the habit of reading. And, being a voracious reader, I think, has been a large enabler to the success I've enjoyed in my career. *Leaders are readers.*

- Ms. Hale was a chemistry teacher at Brownsburg High School, and I had her for two years. She was very demanding, and her exams were not easy. But, she took the time to go through what would be on her tests, and would then thoroughly review the answers to the test afterward. I also remember a show called MacGyver, which was on TV at the time, and which ran from 1985 to 1992. MacGyver was a handyman and had a knack for fixing things unconventionally. His solutions often involved chemistry. Each week, after a show from the previous night, I would ask Ms. Hale how MacGyver did some of the things he did, and she would always take time from class to answer our questions, fully aware that bringing chemistry to life was a good teaching tool.

Secondly, there is no substitute for having an extraordinary work ethic.

My own experience has taught me one thing: "the harder I work, the luckier I get." The most successful people I know were not just talent-rich. They were also extremely hard workers. *I've seen countless examples over the years where people who were more talented and intelligent got out-produced by a person who was more disciplined, more persistent, and simply worked harder.* In my own career, my most successful years I've enjoyed professionally were preceded by working long hours. In many cases, those long hours were nights or on weekends, hours spent that nobody ever saw or appreciated. The reward comes after you've invested the necessary time up-front.

Finally, part of having a high level of character entails a few common sense points to follow.

Perhaps the first thing is *don't ever quit.* Quitting wrinkles the soul. Failure is a natural part of life. Be it sports or business, sometimes you play hard but don't play well. Sometimes you play well, and it simply isn't quite good enough. Maybe you did well, and somebody plays just a little bit better and beats you out. In a business setting, maybe you performed well, but someone else performed just a little bit better and got the promotion. For me, I've never lost sleep over my failures so long as I can look myself in the mirror and know I gave it my best. However, quitting is something that erodes your character, erodes your confidence, erodes your self-esteem. Far better to fail greatly while giving it 100 percent than to quit when the going got tough.

Additionally, if you are a part of a team, *don't tear the entire team down by complaining about your own situation publicly*. Put the team first. There is always plenty of time to work on your own situation. Publicly complaining about your situation makes you look small, weak, selfish, and immature. Complaining is the fastest way to lose the respect of your teammates, whether the setting is a locker room or the board room. Sooner or later, the tide will turn in your situation, and you'll need the backing of your teammates to get where you are trying to go. Developing a reputation as a me-first complainer is not a good way to enlist the help and support of others. As the saying goes, there is no "I" in the word TEAM.

Be persistent. If things are not going the way you would like, you have the ability to change your circumstances (without quitting or blaming others). When faced with adversity, you have choices. You can choose to quit. You can choose to give up. You can choose to blame your coach or boss or someone else. Or, a more productive choice would be to look within. Determine what you need to improve upon, put a plan in place to get better, determine a course of action that brings about the result you desire, and get after it. People who blame others and make excuses become victims of their circumstances. Nothing good can come from this approach. A more productive approach is to take responsibility for your situation and work to improve it. You'll be amazed at how liberating the words "I'm responsible" can be. Or put another way, "if it's to be, it's up to me."

And lastly, *a good sign of character is to keep working, keep playing hard, keep giving it your best even when the end result might already have been decided.* For example, let's say you are in a basketball tournament, and the format is double-elimination. Your team lost the first game, and you are now playing in the consolation game. Don't tank it. Give it 100 percent. You never know who might be watching, and you'll always feel better about yourself afterward, knowing you did your best, knowing you left everything you had to give on the court. The famous football coach Vince Lombardi had a great line, and I'm paraphrasing a little, "a man's finest hour is when he lays exhausted on the field of battle."

A Final Thought on Character

Your reputation is merely what others think of you. Your *character is what you do when you think nobody is looking.* If you're not sure about what you are about to do, ask yourself a simple question: "Would I be comfortable if my actions were on the front page of the newspaper or splattered all over the internet?" If your answer is no, then don't do it. In the business world, I've seen countless people spend more time cultivating a perception of themselves that, in many cases, is not accurate. If they spent as much time and effort working to become someone, instead of acting like someone to build a false perception of themselves, they might actually accomplish something.

Here is one of my favorite poems.

Don't Quit

When things go wrong, as they sometimes will,
When the road you're trudging seems all uphill,
When funds are low and the debts are high,
And you want to smile but you have to sigh,
When care is pressing you down a bit,
Rest if you must, but don't you quit.

Life is queer with its twists and turns,
As every one of us sometimes learns,
And many a failure turns about,
When he might have won if he'd stuck it out.
Don't give up, though the pace seems slow –
You may succeed with another blow.

Often the goal is nearer than
It seems to a faint and faltering man;
Often the struggler has given up
When he might have captured the victor's cup,
And he learned too late, when the night slipped down,
How close he was to the golden crown.

Success is failure turned inside out –
The silver tint of the clouds of doubt,
And you never can tell how close you are –
It may be near when it seems afar;
So stick to the fight when you're hardest hit –
It's when things seem worst that you mustn't quit.

John Greenleaf Whittier

A Collection of Thoughts

Life Lessons

- The old cliché works: "A quitter never wins, and a winner never quits."

- Character counts—more people are watching your every move than you realize, and people appreciate an extraordinary work ethic, persistence, and a positive attitude. How else could a second-stringer on a below .500 basketball team be presented with an award from an entire town?

- More often than not, you can expect to be rewarded for doing the right thing.

- If you've made a commitment to something, then remember people are counting on you. See it through to its completion, even if it's not the easiest thing to do for you personally.

- If you are a part of a team, don't tear the entire team down by publicly complaining about your own situation. Put the team first. There is always time to go to work on your own situation privately.

- Your reputation is what others think of you, which in many cases is not accurate. Your character is what you do when you think nobody is looking. Character is far more important than reputation. Character is the purest thing there is. *Never sell out your own character. It's not for sale at any time, to anyone, at any price.*

Youth Athletics and Character

Before we move on, let me make a few comments on youth athletics. It's important to note for parents who have kids participating in sports to remember the real purpose in athletics is it helps you learn life lessons and helps prepare you for life. Many parents put an enormous amount of pressure on their kids to play sports, to perform well, to participate in travel teams at a young age, and so forth.

My guess is many parents believe their child has a good chance to receive an athletic scholarship to play in college. And, just maybe, if they work hard enough, they might have a chance to play professionally someday. I've often wondered how many parents have asked their child if they enjoy playing all of the sports their parents have signed them up for. Or, if the child does like to play, are they really good enough? While I would never put a damper on a child's dream, parents should be realistic about their child's chances.

Statistically speaking, the odds are very slim that a child will go on to play in college, much less professionally. The following table provides percentages across several different sports for how many high school athletes go on to play collegiately and professionally.

Student Athletes	Men's Basketball	Women's Basketball	Football	Baseball	Men's Soccer
% High School to College	2.9%	3.15%	5.8%	5.6%	5.7%
% College to Pro	1.3%	1.0%	2.0%	10.5%	1.9%
% High School to Pro	0.03%	0.02%	0.09%	0.5%	0.08%

Source: National Collegiate Athletic Association (NCAA). Estimated Probability of Competing in Athletics Beyond the High School Interscholastic Level.

What these statistics tell you is only one in 16,000 high school athletes will attain a professional career in sports. To stick with my basketball theme, this means that out of 10,000 high school basketball players, only three will make it to the NBA.

Why mention this? Because it is important for student athletes and their parents to keep athletics in the proper perspective. If Johnny strikes out in the bottom of the seventh inning or commits an error that costs his team a win, this is not the end of the world. It's just the end of one game. Sure, Johnny will be disappointed, but parents shouldn't make this out to be such a big deal that it becomes a traumatic experience for their son. The real value of participating in athletics is there are life lessons to be learned. There are many parallels to participating in athletics and participating in "the game of life."

Life Lessons from Participating in Athletics

Below are a few lessons that I think are valuable and transferrable from athletics to life.

Have Fun

For starters, playing sports should be fun. Don't ever forget this one. If you're a child, or even in high school, you should enjoy playing, or you shouldn't be doing it. The parallel to life can be found in the importance of choosing your professional career. If you choose a job or profession that doesn't get you excited, that you don't care for very much, then you are likely to be fairly mediocre at it. I've never seen someone, in any endeavor, that was good at something that they really didn't like. There are many reasons to play sports, but the number one reason to play is that you have fun doing it. If you don't enjoy what you're doing or the sport you are playing, then find another activity (or job) that you do enjoy. If it is a sport, finish the season. If you've made a commitment to a group, you owe it to them to finish what you start.

Learn Discipline

Participating in athletics teaches several things that will be useful in life.

- **Must be on time**—You can't be late for practice and expect to play. The same is true in your work life. If you don't show up or don't show up on time, you don't get paid.

- **Work ethic**—There is a direct link between working hard and getting results. This is true individually and collectively. This is a critical discovery. If you don't like the role you're playing on your team, or you aren't getting to play as much as you'd like, you have the choice to practice more to get better. As you get better, you will ultimately end up playing more. *If you put more in, you will get more out.* This is true in almost anything. You will find this is especially true in a professional setting. If you want a job promotion or a pay raise, you must first produce more. Go earn it, and it will come.

- **Hustle**—While on the field or court, give it 110 percent. Victory favors the team that plays the hardest. Examples include such things as diving for loose balls or sprinting back on defense. Hustle will help you in your professional career also. People who arrive a little earlier than everybody else, stay a little later than everybody else, put in the extra time at home by reading in their chosen field and studying their craft (be it accounting, sales, managing) tend to get ahead at a much faster rate than the average worker. Famous author and motivational speaker Brian Tracy has a saying, "It's what you do after you do what you're expected to do, that counts."

Meet Many People

Another benefit of playing sports is you get to meet a lot of people. By participating in sports, or any other organized extracurricular activity for that matter, you are exposed to dramatically more people than simply going to school. You get to know classmates even better when you are playing with them. One of my classmates growing up was a guy named Brent Kiefer. As I'm writing this chapter, I'm 45 years old. I first met Brent when we were 11, playing against each other in Little League. As we grew, we were ultimately teammates in junior high and high school, and remain in contact to this day. You also get to know kids you compete against. To this day, there are several guys I remember that I played against growing up. Living in Brownsburg, we played many county schools that were nearby. Two guys I got to know over the years were Rick Kuster from Lebanon and Eric Clark from Tri-West. A couple of good guys, and two really good athletes.

Learn that Role Players Are Important

Within every team, there are roles to play. To use a baseball analogy, not everyone can bat fourth and pitch. Or in basketball, there is only one leading scorer. It doesn't matter if we are talking about a sales team, operations team, football team, or basketball team—there are roles to play. Within a sales team, some people are better presenters than others. Some are good at cracking into new accounts, and some aren't. In a basketball setting, some are good shooters, some are good defensive players, and some are good rebounders. The point is that not everyone can serve the exact same role and have the team be successful.

One of the best examples I've seen of this came in 1987. Legendary college basketball coach Bob Knight was a genius at making sure everyone understood their role on the team. He was coaching Indiana University's basketball team and had one of the best shooters in the country that year in Steve Alford. However, Steve Alford was not the fastest or quickest guy on the court. He needed help to get his shot off. Enter Brian Sloan. Brian Sloan wasn't particularly fleet of foot either. He was about 6'8" tall, had a broad body, and was more of a rebounder than a scorer. Despite being a fairly average athlete for this level, Brian Sloan found his role on the team. He became a screener for Alford and was relentless at it. In basketball, a screen is when you shield a defender from the offensive player (or block them), so your teammate can get open.

Through Sloan's selfless efforts at screening, something that doesn't show up in the stats book, Alford became one of the leading scorers in the country, and Indiana went on to a 30-4 record that year, won the Big Ten Conference, and won the National Championship. While not the leading scorer, Brian Sloan played a huge part in Indiana's success that year. Brian Sloan did end up getting some recognition for his role. Dick Vitale, a famous basketball announcer, called Sloan the best screener in the country that year. Does Indiana win the National Championship that year without Steve Alford? No way. But it's also not likely they win it without a solid role player like Brian Sloan.

Value Teamwork

You've heard the cliché that there is no "I" in the word TEAM. This is very true. There will be times when you have to subordinate your own goals for the good of the team. We discussed this in the previous section regarding the value of role players. When people are selfish and only concerned with their own success, rest assured the team won't succeed. There is a truism in life that "the tide raises all boats." Putting the team first will earn you people's respect, even if it isn't obvious at the time. And, as the team achieves, individuals achieve as well. We see this in sports all the time. A National Football League (NFL) team goes on to win the Super Bowl; and then after the season, a bunch of players are either getting richer contract extensions with their own team (with guaranteed money), or getting much richer contracts from another team via free agency. Putting the team first almost always pays off.

Play by the Rules

In sports, if you don't follow the rules, you get penalized. Penalties are costly. Bob Knight had a great saying: "Victory favors the team that makes the fewest mistakes." In the NFL, if you break a rule that could cause harm to another player, you face the possibility of fines or suspension. In life, the same thing applies. Play hard. Play to win. But play fair and within the rules. You will go further in life doing it the right way.

We mentioned Pete Rose earlier. Rose is the all-time hits leader in Major League Baseball, and as a result, his accomplishments on the field would easily qualify him for the Hall of Fame—first ballot, in fact. However, Rose is not in the Hall of Fame because he broke a cardinal rule of baseball—he bet on baseball while managing the Cincinnati Reds late in his career. He broke a rule and has paid a big-time price for it. To be transparent, I'm a Pete Rose fan. I think Pete Rose, *the player*, should be in the Hall of Fame because Pete Rose didn't bet on baseball as a player. That said, Pete Rose, *the manager*, did bet on baseball and therefore deserved the ban he received.

Why? He broke the rule on wagering on baseball, a cardinal sin in Major League Baseball.

Learn How to Win/Lose Graciously

Winning graciously in sports is akin to learning how to deal with success in your professional career. My dad always used to tell me never to brag. "If you are good, everybody will know. You don't need to tell them." Besides, bragging makes you look small and insecure. If you have a tremendous game, don't run around bragging about it. Simply say "thank you" when someone says "good game" to you.

Conversely, you don't want to be a bad sport when you lose. If your team gets beat, don't storm off the court or field, blame your teammates or referees, or throw your helmet. This only makes you look small and immature. Hold your head up, shake the other team's hands, and tell them "good game."

Also, you have to learn to accept that not all things are fair. Sometimes your coach doesn't play you as much as he should. Sometimes a referee makes a bad call that can impact the outcome of a game. The same kinds of things happen in life. In the short run, outcomes in life are frequently not fair. But, if you work hard and honestly, the cream will eventually rise. Over the long haul, you will get what you deserve, good or bad. You will ultimately get what you've earned.

Integrity

Webster defines integrity as an unimpaired condition, soundness, honesty, and sincerity. My dad defines having integrity as being able to be counted on to get a job or task done, regardless of how big or small, and regardless of who is watching. And just as important, integrity means being able to be counted on consistently.

Always guard your integrity as if your life depends on it. Your personal integrity is not for sale at any price, for any accomplishment, at any time, to anyone.

Along similar lines, my dad also had a pet saying: "Do what you say you're going to do." If he asked me to take the trash out, and I replied, "I will after dinner," he would not allow me to get comfortable on the couch watching TV after dinner until I had done what I said I would do.

There were times when I was growing up, I thought my dad used to make a big deal about rather small things. Who cares when I take the trash out, I would think to myself, so long as it gets done. As I got older, I began to realize there was a purpose to my dad's methods. He was instilling in me things like discipline, doing what you say you're going to do, and forming good work habits. Developing good habits at an early age goes a long way.

I began to notice around the age of ten that my dad worked long hours. He would frequently go into the office on a Saturday morning or bring work home and work late in the evenings. He took pride in doing his job in an exemplary fashion and made a habit of doing what he was paid to do, plus a little more.

I recently read a book entitled *212 Degrees* by Sam Parker and Mac Anderson. The premise of the book is centered around the idea that to get ahead, you need to put in a little bit more consistently. The authors use the example of how at 211 degrees, water is merely extremely hot. At 212 degrees, water boils. And with boiling water comes steam. And steam can power a locomotive. That single degree makes all the difference.

I began my career with Xerox Corporation in January 1992. My first job was as a Production Supervisor. The team I inherited was not performing very well. Xerox measured quality very closely, and the day I took on this responsibility, we ranked eighth out of eight teams in our region.

Some months into the job, I began doing some things without even really thinking about it. For example, I was putting in long hours. A typical day for me began around 7:00 a.m. and didn't end until around 7:00 p.m., and that was assuming we didn't have any major problems that day. I tended to spend a lot of time on the production floor, helping complete jobs, observing our staff, and performing quality checks. Thus, the administrative part of the job continually took a back seat as the week wore on. So, I began to go into the office on Saturday mornings to catch up, where I could have a few hours of uninterrupted work time. What's my point? Part of having a high level of integrity is doing whatever is necessary to get the job done. When you are a part of a team, people are counting on you.

I remember driving into work one fall Saturday morning, in 1992, I think, and realized how much I was like my dad. When I was growing up, he didn't talk much about his career or what he felt was important to be successful. It wasn't until I began my own career that he began to give me advice on how to deal with people and how to deal with different situations. What I realized that fall morning, perhaps for the first time, is how much my dad had influenced me and my thinking. In many ways, he had influenced me without ever uttering a single word. There is no better definition of leadership than being able to influence people through your actions, without having to say anything.

The most effective leaders lead by example. You've probably heard the saying "walk softly and carry a big stick." In my dad's case, I think he did both. However, the point is if you are in a leadership or parental role, you are being watched far more often and far more closely than you realize. If you want to set a good example, make sure the original is worth copying (no Xerox pun intended).

One final comment on integrity is worth mentioning. *In the battle between the rock and the stream, the stream always wins, not due to strength, but due to persistence.* Truer words were never spoken. A big part of integrity is not giving up at the first sign of trouble. Things will not always go your way. Sometimes life will throw you a curveball just when you think you are close to reaching your goal. It is almost as if nature wants to test you one final time to see if you really want to achieve whatever it is you are aiming at. Successful people keep going regardless of how tough the sledding. "When the going gets tough, the tough get going" is an old saying that will serve you well.

The following story is also a good read regarding, arguably, our nation's all-time greatest leader.

Any Time You Feel Like Quitting

Throughout your career, perhaps you'll remember this story of one of our people:

He failed in business in 1831.

He ran as a state legislator and lost in 1832.

He tried business again in 1833 and failed again.

His sweetheart died in 1835.

He had a nervous breakdown in 1836.

He ran for state elector in 1840 after he regained his health.

He was defeated for Congress in 1843, defeated again for Congress in 1848, defeated when he ran for the Senate in 1855, and defeated for Vice President of the United States in 1856.

He ran for the Senate again in 1858 and lost.

A Collection of Thoughts

This man never quit.

He kept trying until the last.

In 1860, this man, Abraham Lincoln, was elected President of the United States.

Life Lessons

- There can be no second effort without first giving 100 percent effort.

- Do what you say you're going to do.

- A man that can't be trusted with small matters will never be trusted with large ones.

- Vince Lombardi said it best, so no paraphrasing is necessary: "But I firmly believe that any man's finest hour—his greatest fulfillment to all he holds dear—is that moment when he has worked his heart out in a good cause and lies exhausted on the field of battle—victorious."

- If you're in a leadership role, always make sure the original is worth copying.

- Never, ever give up.

CHAPTER

MANAGING YOUR FINANCES
GO AGAINST THE GRAIN

As your career advances, and it surely will, you will likely begin to make an above-average income. Regardless of how much income you earn, how much you keep is just as important, if not more so, than how much you earn. Many call the difference between the two disposable income. Thus, you will need to spend some time thinking about how you will manage your money.

One of the most important habits you can get into is to develop the habit of *delayed gratification*. Getting in the habit of "paying yourself first," in terms of savings and investing, is critically important.

Paying Yourself First

By paying yourself first, I mean before you pay any of your monthly living expenses, you divert money automatically into savings and investment accounts. Once you get into this habit, you won't miss the money. And by starting early, you get time working for you. We will go into "compound annual growth rate" in more detail later in the chapter. For now, a brief description is that compound growth, or compound interest, is when interest is added to the principal of a deposit or loan so that the added interest also earns interest from then on. This addition of interest to the principal is called compounding.

Famous 20th century scientist Albert Einstein is sometimes credited with saying, "Compound interest is the eighth wonder of the world. He who understands it, earns it. He who doesn't, pays it. It's one of the most powerful forces in the universe."

Young adults tend to spend everything they make, plus a little more. In many instances, their spending habits are an attempt to keep up with friends or neighbors. This is where a value system comes into play. It's important to know what you're trying to accomplish before you make an important decision. By defining what is important to you, up front, then it becomes much easier to live your life in accordance with a plan versus making random, haphazard decisions. Remember, if you don't have values, then you will begin to follow someone else's.

This philosophy is especially true when it comes to money. Without a plan and clearly defined financial goals, young adults will buy big screen TVs, stereos, clothes, expensive cars, and procrastinate on important things like short-term savings and long-term savings for retirement. In many instances, young adults pay for these items with credit cards. They think they can pay the minimum amount and carry a balance. No big deal, right? Wrong. Credit card companies are typically charging 15%–18% interest on the balance you are carrying. Paying this level of interest is a colossal mistake, and makes it extraordinarily difficult to build wealth. Rather than taking on credit card debt, do without until you can pay cash. And, don't reduce your disciplined approach to "pay yourself first" in the process.

Regardless of how much money you earn, it is critical that you get into the regular habit of *saving* and *investing*. Getting into the habit of paying yourself first will pay huge dividends later in life (no pun intended). Also, the earlier you start, the better off you will be. *Time is on your side when you're a young adult, so you want to get time working for you as quickly as possible.*

The Power of Time

To illustrate the power of time, let's review an example. Let's say John Doe begins investing $3,000 per year at the age of 20. This is a mere $250 per month. John continues to invest $3,000 per year for the next 10 years, and then he stops investing at the age of 30. Historically, investments in the stock market have earned an average rate of return of 8%. So, John Doe has invested $30,000 after 10 years ($3,000 x 10 years). At an 8% return, this $30,000 investment is now worth $47,000 at age 30.

Now, let's assume John stops investing but doesn't touch his principal of $47,000. He continues to invest this amount, receiving an average rate of return of 8%, for the next 30 years. When John turns 60, his $47,000 is now worth $472,000. **Allow me to belabor the point: his $30,000 investment is now worth $472,000**. How is that possible? Persistence and time, nothing more.

Comparatively, let's say John has a friend from high school named Jane Smith. *Jane waits until she is 30 to begin investing*, a full 10 years after John started. Jane invests the same $3,000 per year, but she invests from age 30 to age 60. Jane earns the same 8% return that John earns. Jane invests for 30 years, so her contribution is $90,000 ($3,000 x 30 years). When Jane turns 60, how much do you think her investment is worth? Since Jane contributed three times as much as John ($90,000 vs. $30,000), she accumulates three times as much, *right*?

Wrong. As the following table illustrates, John's money was working for him an additional 10 years compared to Jane, who didn't begin investing until she was 30. That extra 10 years made an enormous difference.

	John Doe	Jane Smith
Annual amount invested	$3,000	$3,000
Age of initial investment	20	30
Number of years contributing	10	30
Value of portfolio at the age of 30	$47,000	$0
Total amount contributed	$30,000	$90,000
Value of portfolio at the age of 60 **(8% average return)**	**$472,000**	**$367,000**
Annual withdrawals	$42,000	$42,000
Money will last	30 Years	15 Years

John contributed $60,000 less to his portfolio than Jane ($90,000 - $30,000), yet accumulated $105,000 more. How is this possible? Because John's money worked for him for a total of 40 years, whereas Jane's money was only working for her for 30 years. That 10-year difference made a huge difference. The moral of the story is you can't start too soon to begin saving and investing.

Saving vs. Investing

The preceding example was centered on investing. This is a good time to review the differences between saving and investing, as many people use these terms interchangeably without understanding the difference.

Savings typically is used for short-term use cases and is money that you use to pay living expenses. It also needs to be in very liquid financial instruments so that you have ready access to your cash for purposes such as funding a family vacation or accumulating money for the down payment of a new car.

Investing is a much longer time horizon. Investments typically are used for such things as retirement, your kid's college education, or perhaps purchasing a vacation home down the road. Additionally, unlike savings, investing contains an element of risk. The following table, at a high level, provides a brief synopsis of the differences between saving and investing.

	Saving	Investing
Risk	Low to none	Moderate to high
Reward/Expected rates of return	0.5%–3.0%	5.0% + The long-term average rate of return in the stock market has been 8% since World War II
Duration in time	Short term, usually three years or less	Long term, typically five years or more, and can be decades
Use cases	Medium-sized items, such as family vacations, down payments on cars, or small home remodeling projects

Living expenses:
• Mortgage
• Utilities
• Food
• Clothing | Large items, such as retirement, funding future college expenses, or purchasing a new home |
| Instruments | Checking/Savings accounts, accounts, short-term money market accounts, CDs | Stocks, Bonds, Mutual Funds |

Wealth Preservation

Now that we have a few definitions out of the way, let's get into a little more detail. Managing your finances is largely about building wealth. As we saw above, one of the most important aspects of building wealth is time. Then once you have some wealth, *wealth preservation* becomes critically important. There are a few things to be aware of in regard to preserving wealth, as they can be *barriers* to wealth preservation:

- Market losses
- Taxes
- Brokerage fees

These three concepts have helped shape my thinking dramatically over the years as it relates to money and wealth accumulation. Let's discuss each one and provide a few examples. Then at the end of the chapter, I'll provide what I believe to be a good response to these wealth-preservation barriers.

Conventional Wisdom

Before we continue, let's review what many believe to be no-brainer, *conventional wisdom* concepts regarding funding your wealth goals and funding retirement:

- Max out your 401K contributions.

- Take advantage of every tax-deferred instrument you can.

- Buy term life insurance instead of whole life insurance because it has lower premiums. Then, invest the difference in the stock market.

- Invest in the stock market, where you will get a higher rate of return.

- Invest in mutual funds to ensure you are diversified.

I read a very good book a few years ago titled *Safe Money Millionaire* by Brett Kitchen and Ethan Kap. They stated some very interesting and alarming statistics:

- Half of all households headed by workers aged 55 to 64 have less than $88,000 in retirement accounts.

- The average American household with at least one credit card has nearly $11,000 in credit card debt.

- Trillions of dollars have evaporated from 401K accounts over the last couple of market corrections.

- Of those between 46 and 64, 71% admit they are worried about having enough money for retirement.
- The average American is paying up to 34.5% of their after-tax income straight to interest.
- In 2010, every 3 months 250,000 new homes went into foreclosure.

You will hear many pundits and brokers state that, on average, the stock market will produce an 8% return over the long run. Sure, there are ups and downs, and the occasional market correction, but over the long-haul, this is where you will earn the highest returns, or so goes the theory. So, let's take a closer look. Below is commentary on the three barriers mentioned earlier (market losses, taxes, brokerage fees) to be aware of as it relates to wealth preservation.

Barrier 1: Market Losses

Let's go back to John Doe in our previous example. Let's say John starts with $5,000 and decides to invest in the stock market. He gets lucky, and his mutual fund increases by 100% in one year, a very strong return. His balance is now $10,000.

The following year, let's say the market doesn't do well, and his mutual fund drops by 50%. In year three, the market goes up by 100%, and then in year 4, the market drops 50% again. How does this look over time?

Year	Market Performance	Beginning Balance	Ending Balance
1	+ 100%	$5,000	$10,000
2	-50%	$10,000	$5,000
3	+ 100%	$5,000	$10,000
4	-50%	$10,000	$5,000

In this rudimentary example, the market averaged a 25% return over four years (+200% in gains, -100% in losses, spread over four years), yet John's money is right back to where he started. He made $0 in the market. Now, take that same $5,000, and if you invested in a no-risk instrument at a 6% annual return, you would end up with $6,312, a net gain of $1,312. **How does a 6% return net more than a 25% average return over four years?** The answer is because the 25% return example loses its principal when the market goes down. In the 6% example, we haven't put our principal at risk. It's difficult to grow your money if your principal shrinks every time the market declines.

Now, you might say the market doesn't swing that wildly, at least not in that short of a period of time. I would submit to you it can, and often does. However, that's fine. Let's use different numbers. Let's start with the same $5,000 we began with in the previous example. In year one, the market increases by 20%. Then in year 2, it contracts by 10%. In year three, we recover our year two loss. Then in year 4, the market contracts by 5%. These types of returns/losses are not just within the realm of reason, but commonplace. So, how does this look?

Year	Market Performance	Beginning Balance	Ending Balance
1	+20%	$5,000	$6,000
2	-10%	$6,000	$5,400
3	+10%	$5,400	$5,940
4	-5%	$5,940	$5,643

Good news—you gained $643. Again, let's take a closer look. In this example, a stockbroker would tell you the stock market approach produced a 15% return (30% in gains and 15% in losses). However, this was spread over four years. So the average return was really only 3.75% (15% / 4), yet you only made $643. If we had invested the same $5,000, and made 3.75% compounded annually, then we would have made $794. The table below illustrates the differences.

Year	Market Performance (15% Market)	Beginning Balance - $5,000	Net Gain/(Loss)	Market Performance (3.75% Fixed)	Beginning Balance - $5,000	Net Gain/(Loss)
1	+20%	$6,000	$1,000	+3.75%	$5,188	$188
2	-10%	$5,400	($600)	+3.75%	$5,383	$195
3	+10%	$5,940	$540	+3.75%	$5,585	$202
4	-5%	$5,643	($297)	+3.75%	$5,794	$209
Net			$643			$794

How did a 3.75% fixed return beat the stock market approach?

A Collection of Thoughts

First, stock brokers tend to talk in averages. An average return is not the same as a compound annual growth rate (CAGR). In our example above, the market produced a return of 15% (20-10 + 10-5). This is a mathematical calculation. However, had you realized a 15% CAGR, then you would have earned $3,745, not $643.

Secondly, the difference between these two examples is that in the market example, we are putting our entire principal at risk. When the market goes up, our balance goes up. But, when the market goes down, our entire portfolio goes down also. If the market goes down 5% in one year, we have to gain a 5% return in the following year just to get back to even. In our fixed example, we are not putting our principal at risk. Our money grows regardless of what the market does. Our money is compounding, which means that we are earning interest on both our principal and the accrued interest over time. This is a very important point to understand.

Additionally, in an age of real-time analytics and day traders, there can be wild swings in the markets from one day to the next. Some might argue these trends can and do manipulate the market to provide professional traders the ability to make money when the market goes up (calls) or down (puts). Briefly, a call gives the owner of the option contract the right, but not the obligation, to buy a specified amount of an underlying security at a specified price within a specified period of time. A put is the opposite. It gives the owner of the option contract the right, but not the obligation, to sell a specified amount of an underlying security at a specified price within a specified period of time. Call option contract owners are betting their securities are going to increase in value, and put option contract owners are betting their securities are going to decrease in value.

These are strategies deployed by professional traders to protect themselves against the market moving against them, and to potentially make money whether the market goes up or down. Now, don't get me wrong. I'm not stating you shouldn't be investing in the stock market. There is a time and place for the stock market, but not, in my humble opinion, for your *entire* retirement portfolio.

Barrier 2: Taxes

There are only two certainties in life: death and taxes. As you reach adulthood, you will begin to see how big of a bite taxes take out of your income. We pay taxes on a myriad of things:

- Federal income tax
- State income tax
- City/County tax
- Sales tax on products you purchase
- Social Security tax
- Medicare/Medicaid tax
- Estate tax—that's right. You can get taxed even in death!
- Interest tax—you pay taxes on the interest you earn in savings/checking accounts, as that counts as income.
  - So let me get this straight. I paid taxes on my income. I put what's left over in the bank, and I get taxed on the interest earned? Yep! Isn't that like getting taxed twice on the same income? Yep!
- Capital gains tax—if you buy stock, and it increases in value, and then you sell it, you pay taxes on the gain.
  - So let me get this one straight. I paid taxes on my income. I take some of what is left over and buy stock. If the stock goes up and I sell it, I have to pay taxes on the gain too? Yep! Isn't that like getting taxed on the same income twice? Yep!
  - So what happens if I buy stock, and it goes down in value. Do I get to write down my loss on my taxes? Nope. You pay taxes effectively twice, with no downside protection. Makes a lot of sense, right?

To build wealth, you have to have strategies in place to minimize your tax burden. As I say that, I'm not talking about cheating. I'm talking about legal ways to protect your hard-earned money. We will address specific strategies at the end of this chapter.

Earlier in the chapter we mentioned one conventional wisdom approach to building wealth for retirement is to invest in tax deferred instruments such as a 401K. The theory is you want to delay your tax bill as long as you can. And, by the time you retire, you will be making significantly less money so your tax bill will be less. This is worth a second look as well. While on the surface that sounds like a sound strategy, there are a few things to be aware of.

First, during your working life, you are likely to have multiple tax deductions you can leverage legally to reduce your tax bill. That said, many of these itemized deductions will go away when you retire. The list below, as of this writing, is a list of tax deductions that would likely go away once you retire.

- Number of dependents (in my case three)
- Mortgage interest paid on your home
- Interest paid on a home equity line of credit
- Union and/or professional dues related to your job
- Work uniforms or clothing/safety gear related to your job

So what's the point? The point is while your income in retirement is likely to be significantly lower than when you were working, your tax deductions are also going to be quite a bit lower, if not nonexistent.

A *second* thing to keep in mind is tax rates. The following table provides the tax brackets, by income level, for federal income taxes for 2014.

Tax Rate	Single	Married/Joint & Widow(er)	Married/ Separate	Head of Household
10%	$1 to $9,075	$1 to $18,150	$1 to $9,075	$1 to $12,950
15%	$9,076 to $36,900	$18,151 to $73,800	$9,076 to $36,900	$12,951 to $49,400
25%	$36,901 to $89,350	$73,801 to $148,850	$36,901 to $74,425	$49,401 to $127,550
28%	$89,351 to $186,350	$148,851 to $226,850	$74,426 to $113,425	$127,551 to $206,600
33%	$186,351 to $405,100	$226,851 to $405,100	$113,426 to $202,550	$206,601 to $405,100
35%	$405,101 to $406,750	$405,101 to $457,600	$202,551 to $228,800	$405,101 to $432,200
39.6%	over $406,750	over $457,600	over $228,800	over $432,200

As you can see, the top marginal tax rate is currently 39.6%. However, that is rather low based on historical standards. To provide some historical context, the following table contains the bottom and top marginal tax rates over select time periods.

Year	Lowest Marginal Tax Rate	Highest Marginal Tax Rate
2013–2014	10.0 %	39.6 %
2002–2012	10.0 %	38.6 %
1993–1999	15.0 %	39.6 %
1982–1986	0.0 %	50.0 %
1977–1981	0.0 %	70.0 %
1965–1976	14.0 %	70.0 %
1964	16.0 %	77.0 %
1954–1963	20.0 %	91.0 %

Note: This information came from the Tax Foundation, a firm that's been around since 1937.

Given our country has approximately $19 trillion in debt, and growing each year, is it more likely or less likely that tax rates will increase in the future? Our government is very poorly run when it comes to fiscal matters. I would bet dollars to donuts tax rates will increase in the future. So, it is quite possible a tax-deferred strategy could end up causing you to pay more in taxes, not less.

This final comment on taxes, I think, may be the most important. If you are investing in a traditional 401K, and leave that money alone until you retire, you will have presumably accumulated a large amount of gains. *When you begin to withdraw from this account for living expenses, you will get taxed on this as income.* Why? Because you invested on a tax-deferred basis. You weren't taxed on this money up front, so you now need to pay taxes on it as you begin to withdraw. Fair enough.

However, that's not the entire story. Let's say you put away $1,000,000 over your working life, and at the time you retire, your 401K is now worth $1,500,000 inclusive of gains. How much money are you going to end up paying taxes on—$1,000,000 or $1,500,000? You will pay taxes on the entire amount—$1,500,000! Think about that for a moment. *We will pay taxes on the deferred income we set aside, plus 100% of our gains!* And based on our previous tax discussion, we will likely be paying taxes on both the investment principal and all associated capital gains at a higher tax rate. How does that sound?

A Collection of Thoughts

Let's put this revelation into a live example. Assume you invested $5,000 per year over 30 years. At the end of the 30 years, you've invested $150,000. Let's also assume you are in a 33% federal tax bracket, so over that 30-year period, you will have paid $49,500 in taxes. Assuming a rate of return of 6.5%, at the end of 30 years, you will have accumulated $348,854.

Now, let's take that same $5,000 per year, but invest in a traditional 401K (the stock market). We will assume the same 33% tax bracket, the same 6.5% rate of return, and the same 30 year investment period. At the end of 30 years, we will have accumulated $498,018. So, investing in the stock market generated an additional $149,164 ($498,018 - $348,854). This is a no-brainer, right?

Not so fast. Keep in mind that we haven't paid any income taxes on the stock market approach as of yet, as the $5,000 per year investment was on a tax-deferred basis. Once you retire, you will begin to withdraw from this retirement account for living expenses. So, let's assume you withdraw $73,000 per year to live on. At the 33% tax rate, you will be paying $24,090 in taxes each year. Assuming you continue to earn 6.5% on the balance, this money will run out in approximately nine years. Thus, you will have paid $216,810 in taxes. Given we had accumulated $498,018, but paid $216,810 in taxes, we netted $281,208. Therefore, by investing in the stock market, and deferring taxes, we accumulated $67,646 less ($348,854 - $281,208) than had we leveraged a different strategy. This process is summarized in the following table.

	Investments After Taxes	Stock Market – Tax Deferred Investments
Annual Investment	$5,000	$5,000
Investment Duration	30 Years	30 Years
Total Invested Before Return/Taxes	$150,000	$150,000
Rate of Return	6.5%	6.5%
Total Accumulated Including Return	$348,854	$498,018
Tax Rate	33%	33%
Incremental Taxes Due After 30 Years	$0 (we invested on an after-tax basis)	$24,810 x 9 = $216,810
Net Accumulation	$348,854	$281,208

Note: The example above came from the book *Safe Money Millionaire* (a very good read).

There are three takeaways from the preceding example:

1. Investing on a tax-deferred basis does not necessarily net us more money, and it exposes us to additional risks.

2. We have assumed tax rates in the future are the same as what they are today. If they go up, which I suspect they will, then the gap is even greater.

3. Finally, and perhaps most important, we've assumed no significant market correction over this 30-year period. As we have seen, a market correction could substantially impact the size of our portfolio, in that 100% of our portfolio is exposed to risk in a stock market approach. And market corrections do happen, and in many cases happen sharply and quickly.

Barrier 3: Brokerage Fees

The last barrier to wealth preservation is brokerage fees. Brokerage fees are fees we pay professional money managers to manage our portfolio, make recommendations on financial instruments worth investing in, stock picks, and fees to execute trades and buy or sell securities. That seems fair. You can't expect people to work for free. That said, this is yet another expense that gets taken from your portfolio, so it is prudent to shop around a little. I've always been willing to pay a premium for a premium product or service, but these fees can vary wildly. It is not uncommon for brokerage fees to run 1%–3% per month. And like deferred taxes, this is 1%–3% of your entire portfolio, in perpetuity. This adds up over time—big time. The following table provides an illustration based on a portfolio of $500,000.

Portfolio of $500,000	Brokerage Fees: 1 Year	Brokerage Fees: 5 Years	Brokerage Fees: 10 Years	Brokerage Fees: 20 Years	Brokerage Fees: 30 Years
Brokerage Fees: 0.5%	$2,500	$12,500	$25,000	$50,000	$75,000
Brokerage Fees: 1.0%	$5,000	$25,000	$50,000	$100,000	$150,000
Brokerage Fees: 2.0%	$10,000	$50,000	$100,000	$200,000	$300,000
Brokerage Fees: 3.0%	$15,000	$75,000	$150,000	$300,000	$450,000

As you can see, brokerage rates can make a huge difference over time. If we compare brokerage fees of 0.5% versus 3.0%, over time, we could be talking about hundreds of thousands of dollars over our working life (see highlight above). This is not monopoly money; this is real money you are paying. And in our example above, we have assumed no principal increases. Had we assumed annual growth rates to our portfolio, the fees would have been even greater. *You mean I get charged brokerage fees on my portfolio, plus the gains?* Yep. Just like our tax example, there is no such thing as a free lunch. So, it will be worth your time to shop brokerage fee rates. Don't be afraid to pay a premium for a premium level of service, but you will find in many cases brokerage fees can be negotiable and can vary widely from one firm to another.

So What Should I Do with My Money?

Up to this point, I've given you the bad news. *The good news is there are safe ways to save and invest your money.* If you start early, if you have a plan, and if you are disciplined, you can do well financially over your working life. So, how should you spread your money? And at what time intervals? The time of your life is important to keep in mind. For example, when you're young, you really don't need much, if any, life insurance. But if you have children, then you need to make sure they are taken care of. Another example is risk. When you're a young adult, you can afford to take significantly more risk than you can when you're in your 40s or 50s. And if you're in your 60s, 70s, or 80s, you really don't want to be taking any risk at all. Once you reach your 60s and 70s, if not sooner, you should be focused more on wealth preservation and less on growing your portfolio.

Throw Conventional Wisdom Out the Window

At this time I'd like to introduce you to a new concept. *What we're going to talk about is contrary to conventional wisdom*, where you put all of your long-term investment dollars into the stock market, and then buy term life insurance to protect your family in the event something happens to you. Why invest in the stock market? Because everyone knows that is where the highest returns are, right? As we've seen, one problem with this approach is your retirement is entirely dependent on what the market does. You have no control over this, as returns in the market are uncertain and completely out of your control.

Additionally, investing in the stock market, as we saw earlier, ignores market losses, future tax implications, brokerage fees, and exposes your entire portfolio (principal + gains) to market corrections.

This new concept is called Cash Value Life Insurance. A Cash Value Life Insurance policy is a life insurance policy, but it has far more flexibility to it than traditional term insurance. There are many different types of life insurance. However, for discussion purposes, we will briefly discuss Term Life, Traditional Whole Life, and Cash Value Life.

Term Life Insurance

Definition: Term Life Insurance provides a policyholder with coverage for a fixed, finite period of time. Common terms are 10, 15, 20, 25, and 30-year policies. If the policyholder dies, the dependents inherit the value of the policy. For example, with a $1,000,000 policy, your family receives $1,000,000 upon your death.

Pros: Because the majority of term life policies never pay a death benefit, insurance companies can offer them with a much lower premium than other forms of life insurance. If the only thing you're interested in is providing the highest amount of benefit to your family if you die, at the lowest possible cost, then term insurance is a good way to go.

Cons: This policy does not generate wealth, nor is it an asset. You pay a premium, usually monthly or annually, for the term of the policy. Once the term expires, you have nothing to show for it (assuming you didn't die during that term). This is the most likely scenario, statistically speaking. For example, a $1,000,000 policy would cost you $1,200 in annual premiums, and since it is a 30-year policy, then you will have paid $36,000 over the term ($1,200 x 30). If you shell out $36,000, you'd like to have something to show for it, right?

Traditional Whole Life Insurance

Definition: Traditional Whole Life Insurance (sometimes called Permanent Life) pays a benefit to your beneficiaries upon your death. Typically the benefit and the premium are both fixed. Unlike term insurance, this policy is usually in effect for your entire life, not just for a specific term (assuming you are current on your premiums).

Pros: A Whole Life Insurance policy provides some cash value benefit over time based on how much your premium is. The cash value portion is an alternative, not an additional, benefit under the policy. And, unlike Term Insurance, which is worthless upon policy expiration, a Whole Life policy is an asset that can be left for your beneficiaries.

Cons: This type of insurance costs quite a bit more than Term Insurance, as it is for a longer period of time and provides more flexibility than Term Insurance.

Cash Value Life Insurance

Definition: Cash Value Life Insurance policies are also sometimes called Universal Life or Variable Universal Life policies. A Cash Value policy provides life insurance for designated beneficiaries, but also contains a cash value portion that grows over time. When looking at this type of policy, you want to have a policy that maximizes cash growth and minimizes the cost of the life insurance portion. This is what will enable us to finance loans to ourselves should we choose to (more on this later), while still providing life insurance for our beneficiaries.

Pros: Cash Value policies continue throughout your entire life, provided you continue to make your premium payments. Also, the cash value continues to grow on a tax-deferred basis so long as the policy is in full force, and you are current on your payments. Why tax deferred? Because you are putting money in this policy after taxes. *And unlike your 401K, you are not taxed on your gains.* Finally, because there is a cash value component, this is an asset that can be handed down to your beneficiaries on a tax-deferred basis. But, this is also an asset that you can benefit from. With Term Insurance, only your heirs benefit.

Cons: Cash Value policies are quite a bit more expensive than Term Insurance. Additionally, the cash value early in the policy term is not worth a lot. Generally speaking, it can take five to ten years before you can realistically begin drawing upon the cash portion. So once again, it's a good idea to start early.

Cash Value Life Insurance Benefits

It is true that a Cash Value Life Insurance policy costs a lot more than Term Insurance, but it also provides a lot more. Term Life Insurance is less expensive than Cash Value, but it also doesn't have any flexibility, and it is not an asset that grows over time. This is such an important point; let's dive into the benefits in more detail: growth, finance yourself, taxes, asset, and risk.

- **Growth:** This policy is not associated with the stock market in any way, shape, or form. The insurance company is the one guaranteeing the growth rate. Insurance companies have been around for hundreds of years, and they use actuarial tables to know how to provide benefits to their clients and still make some money for themselves. Thus, you can get a guaranteed rate, typically 5%–8%, regardless of what the stock market does.

- **Finance Yourself:** Because this policy has a cash value portion, you can leverage the accumulated cash for big-ticket items, such as for a car, a home remodeling project, or college expenses. Let's say you buy a $30,000 car and take out a regular loan to purchase it. You are likely going to pay 5%–6% in interest on that loan. Over a five-year loan, that $30,000 car likely costs you closer to $35,000, including interest. However, what if instead, you wrote a check for the $30,000 car leveraging your Cash Value policy, and then paid yourself back? The net benefit is three-fold:

  - The cash value portion of your policy (that is the principal), if structured properly, continues to grow as if you never touched it.

  - With a traditional loan, the interest you are paying goes directly to the bank. With a cash value policy, you are paying yourself back. In fact, if you decide to pay yourself back at prevailing interest rates, you are actually increasing the cash value of the policy.

  - If you take out a loan against yourself, there is no approval process to go through, no credit checks, no timetable for when you have to have the loan paid off, and there are no late fees given there is no timetable for payments.

- **Taxes:** Based on today's IRS laws, *life insurance is one of the most protected financial items there is.* Our current tax code (2015 as of this writing) does not penalize or double tax this type of asset. There are multiple benefits:

  - Beneficiaries: When your beneficiaries receive a death benefit, this is not taxable.

  - Growth: As the cash value portion of your policy grows, you are not taxed on the gains. Why? Because we are putting money into this account on an after-tax basis.

– Withdrawals: If you withdraw against your cash value portion of the policy, this does not trigger a taxable event. This is unlike your 401K, where if you take a withdrawal you are immediately taxed as if it were income. And worse, there is usually a penalty if you take a withdrawal before retirement age. How does that sound? *You get taxed and penalized for accessing your own money!* Neither of these is the case with a Cash Value Policy.

- **Asset:** Unlike Term Insurance, a Cash Value policy is an asset that you can use during your lifetime. You can withdraw against it for purchases, you can withdraw against it for retirement, or you can leave it alone. You can also leave it to your heirs as a part of your estate.

- **Risk:** The only risk with this type of policy is if the insurance company goes out of business or defaults. I'm not aware of an insurance company that has defaulted. With traditional stock market investments, as we have seen in our past discussions, your entire portfolio is exposed to market crashes, market corrections, and market downturns.

Term Life Insurance vs. Cash Value Life Insurance

The following table provides a quick summary of the differences between Term Insurance and Cash Value Life Insurance policies.

	Term Life Insurance	Cash Value Life Insurance
Term	Finite period, usually 10, 20, or 30 years	Lasts your entire life
Cash value portion	No	Yes
Cost of premium	Low	Medium to high
Tax implications	None, as this isn't an asset	None, as gains in the cash value portion are not taxable because we are saving on an after-tax basis
Flexibility: Is this an asset whose value accrues?	No	Yes. You can borrow against the cash value, and then repay yourself vs.paying interest to a bank
Does the policy grow?	No	Yes. If structured properly, the principal continues to grow even if you have borrowed against it. It grows as if you never touched it.

	Term Life Insurance	Cash Value Life Insurance
What happens if the market contracts?	Not applicable	Nothing. Your growth and rates of return are not dependent, or in any way associated with the stock market. Gains come from the insurance company, with no risk of loss.
Who benefits?	Only your beneficiaries	You and your designated beneficiaries, as you can use the cash value portion during your life, and the life insurance benefit goes to your beneficiaries upon your death.

Financial Blueprint

So, what's the blueprint? Based on the preceding discussion, I think the following rules of thumb are a good starting point in terms of *what, where, how much,* and in *what time intervals* to spread your money. These suggestions include guidance on:

(1) Savings

(2) Tracking interest

(3) Investing

(4) Life insurance

(5) Cash value life insurance

(1) Savings

Save as much as you can until you get 12 months of living expenses in your savings/checking account. We referred to this earlier as "pay yourself first." You can do this by diverting a fixed amount of money each month, directly from your paycheck, into an emergency account. I would keep this amount in there at all times. This will ensure if you ever had an unexpected emergency or found yourself unemployed, you will have enough money to get through the short-term problem. Conversely, you may stumble across a business or investment opportunity. Make sure you've done your home-work, but having an "emergency fund" could be useful in taking advantage of a unique opportunity as well.

Note: Track your monthly living expenses very closely. You should have a good understanding of where your money is going. By doing this, you'll know exactly how much money 12 months of living expenses require. (What gets measured gets done.)

Once you've achieved the emergency fund goal, I would continue to save 10% of your income. If expenses are tight, which they may well be when you're a young adult, then start with 2% and work your way up from there. Then, each time you get a pay increase, make sure a portion of that pay increase goes toward your savings goal. If you get a 3% pay increase, then bump your savings from 2%–5%, and so on until you get to 10%.

(2) Track Interest (Very Important)

It's a good practice to compare how much money per month you are paying in interest versus how much you are earning in interest. There is *good leverage* to your ability to build wealth if you are earning more in interest than you are paying. This is very difficult to do when you are young and just starting out. You will need to take out a loan for many things as you get started in adult life, such as a car or home. You may also be paying on a student loan from college. However, as your income grows, the percent of your income being paid out in debt should go down, and the gap between interest paid versus interest earned should start to close.

When you get to a point where you're earning more in interest than you are paying, you'll know you are on the right track. *It's been said there are two kinds of people in the world: those who pay interest and those who earn it.* You don't want to wind up being a slave to a lender. At some point, you will want to fall into the latter group—the sooner, the better. Earning more in interest than you are paying is a great way to accelerate wealth creation.

Here are three mortgage examples. One way to minimize interest expense is to get in the habit of paying off loans early, meaning paying them off quicker than the term. The greatest interest savings opportunity there is will be your home mortgage. In Appendix E, at the end of the book, I've included two examples of a traditional mortgage. The tables you see are called amortization schedules. There are a lot of numbers, and they take up a number of pages, but I think this is so important it is worth taking extra time and space to illustrate. *So what is an amortization schedule?* It is a table detailing each periodic payment on a loan. Amortization refers to the process of paying off a loan over time through regular payments. A portion of each payment is for *interest*, while the remaining amount is applied towards the *principal* balance. The percentage of interest versus principal in each payment is determined in an amortization schedule. The schedule differentiates out the portion of the payment that belongs to interest expense and the portion used to retire the debt owed.

- **Example 1: 30-Year Mortgage.** Let's say you buy a home for $300,000, and make a down payment of 20% or $60,000. Day one, you owe the bank $240,000. Let's also assume a 30-year mortgage (360 equal monthly payments) and a fixed interest rate of 5%. Your payment schedule can be found in Appendix E. A few observations:

  - Your fixed monthly payment is $1,288.37. However, for your first payment, only $288.37 of that total is going toward paying down the principal. The remainder is interest (fully 77% of the payment).

  - It isn't until payment 195 of 360, or year 16, until you are paying more in principal than interest.

  - Over the life of the 30-year loan, you will pay $223,813 in interest. **Thus, the $240,000 mortgage actually costs you $463,813**.

- **Example 2: 15-Year Mortgage**. Let's say you buy the same home as in the first example ($300,000 home, 20% down, $240,000 mortgage). However, this time you take out a 15-year mortgage (180 equal monthly payments) at a fixed interest rate of 4%. Given the term is less, the interest rate is also lower. Your payment schedule can be found in Appendix E. A few observations for this example:

- Your fixed monthly payment is now $1,775.25. However, for your first payment, $975.25 of that total is going toward paying down the principal. The remainder is interest (only 45% of the payment in this example).

- In this example, *you are paying more in principal than in interest from day one.*

- Over the life of the 15-year loan, you will end up paying $79,544 in interest. Thus, the $240,000 mortgage will actually cost you $319,544. Note: By paying the loan off in 15 years versus 30, you save $144,269 in interest ($223,813 - $79,544).

- Based on this example, I would submit to you nobody can afford a 30-year mortgage. Imagine investing that same $144,269 in a fixed annuity spread over the 15 years in time savings, at a 6% rate of return. *Instead of paying $144,269 in interest, you would have accumulated $345,749.* **This is a delta of $490,018—phenomenal leverage!**

- **Example 3: 5-Year Car Loan.** For our third example, we'll review a much smaller loan amount. Let's say you buy a car for $36,000 and put 20% as a down payment or $6,000. Thus, you have a $30,000 loan. Let's also assume a 5-year loan (60 months) at a 6% interest rate. Your payment schedule can be found in Appendix E. A few observations:

– Your fixed monthly payment is $579.98.

– You end up paying $4,769 in interest over the life of the loan. Thus, the $30,000 loan actually costs you $34,769.

How do I reduce my interest expenses? Let's go back to our 30-year mortgage example. Let's say I can't afford the monthly payment on a 15-year mortgage, so I take out a 30-year loan. You can still pay a loan off early. For example, let's say in month 2, you want to make a double payment. You would pay 2 x $1,288.37, or $2,576.74—right? Wrong. If you are making extra payments against any loan, the second payment is *principal only*. You are saving the interest portion of the payment. Thus, a second payment in month 2 is as follows:

Month 2 Payment:	$1,288.37
Month 3 (Extra Payment—Principal only):	$ 290.78
Total Payment:	**$1,579.15**

What did we just do? We made two payments and saved the interest in month 3, or $997.59. Let's take this out again. Let's say you get a bonus at work, and you want to make four payments in Month 12 of your loan. It would look as follows:

Month 12 Payment:	$1,288.37
Month 13 (Extra Payment— Principal only):	$ 303.12
Month 14 (Extra Payment— Principal only):	$ 304.39
Month 15 (Extra Payment— Principal only):	$ 305.65
Total Payment:	**$2,201.53**

In this case, we saved the interest in month 13 ($985.25), month 14 ($983.98), and month 15 ($982.72), or a total of $2,951.95. As you can see, you can save tens of thousands of dollars over the life of a loan by making extra payments. As you look at the amortization schedule, you'll also notice that over time the amount of your fixed payment that goes toward principal increases, and the amount that goes toward interest decreases, even though the total payment remains fixed. Thus, it is more impactful to make extra payments early in a loan vs. late in a loan. For example, if you wanted to make an extra payment in month 300, the interest saved is only $286.64—not insignificant, but a far cry from what we saved in months 13–15.

Note: You should keep an amortization schedule for every loan you take out, and systematically pay the loan off early by making extra (principal only) payments. *By paying off loans early, you will save hundreds of thousands of dollars over your working life.*

(3) Investing

As we've seen from previous examples, get started early. When I was working for Xerox, I began investing a mere 2% into a 401K when I was 23. I really didn't miss the 2%, and as I received pay increases, I increased my investing rates to 5%, 8%, 10%, until I was maximizing what the government allows you to invest on a tax-deferred basis. By the time I was 30, I had accumulated about $70,000 without really missing the money that was being set aside. Invest 5%–10% of your annual, pre-tax income to fund long-term financial goals, perhaps the most pressing being retirement.

Many companies have matching programs with their 401K plans. For example, they may match up to 6%. What this means is if you invest 6%, the company will match your 6%. Thus, your 6% equates to 12%. This is free money. I would make sure, at the very least, you are taking advantage of any company matching that is offered.

(4) Life Insurance

This financial expense is highly dependent on your family situation. If you are single, one could argue you don't need life insurance at all. In my case, at the time of this writing, I am married with three small children (14, 11, and 6 years old). I think maintaining a policy (or policies) that would replace 10 times your annual income is roughly right. Should something happen to you at an early age, the last thing you want your wife worrying about is how she will make ends meet financially, especially if there are kids involved.

(5) Cash Value Life Insurance

I would begin saving as much as you can as early as you can in a cash value life insurance policy. Begin with whatever you can afford, even if it is only $25 or $50 per month. You want to increase this until you get up to $10,000 per year. As was mentioned earlier, starting early is very important. It can take 5 to 10 years before you build up a generous cash value portion. Even if a small amount, get started early. You can always increase the monthly amount as your income increases.

Financial Guidance Summary

The guidance discussed in the Financial Blueprint section, over your working life, might look something like the summary in the following table.

Your Age	Savings/ Checking	Investments Tax Deferred	Investments Cash Value	Life Insurance	Rationale/ Logic
22	Save 2% of your annual income and don't touch it unless you have an emergency.	Defer 2% of your annual income, before taxes, into a company sponsored 401K.	Save $25 per month/ $600 per year.	None (assuming you have no children).	Get in the habit early of paying yourself first. Also, maximize any matching your company provides in a 401K.
25	Save 5% of your annual income until you get to 12 months' worth of living expenses. This is Priority # 1.	Defer 5% of your annual income, before taxes, into a company sponsored 401K.	Save $50 per month/ $600 per year	None (assuming you have no children).	Ratchet up your "pay yourself first" from 5%–10%.
30	Save 10% of your annual income. Your expenses may be going up at this point. Adjust your savings rate to maintain 12 months' worth of living expenses.	Defer 10% of your annual income until you reach the maximum government allotment (currently $18,000 per year).	Save $250 per month/ $3,000 per year.	5X your annual income if you have one child.	Begin saving in a Cash Value Life Insurance Policy that will provide more flexibility for you, with less risk. Regarding your 401K, make sure to take advantage of company matching.

continued

Your Age	Savings/ Checking	Investments Tax Deferred	Investments Cash Value	Life Insurance	Rationale/ Logic
35	Save 10% of annual income.	Defer 15% of your annual income.	Save $10,000 per year.	8X your annual income if you have two children.	The Cash Value and Life Insurance policies may well be connected.
40	Save 10% of annual income.	Defer 10% of annual income.	Increase saving to $1,000 per month, or $12,000 per year.	10X your annual income if you have three children, maybe more if your kids go to private schools.	Notice we have reduced the 401K investment to fund our increase in the Cash Value policy. At this point you want to begin to think about wealth preservation.
45	Save 10% of annual income.	Defer 5% or at least enough to maximize any company matching.	Increase saving to $1,500 per month if you can.	10X your annual income if you have three children, maybe more if your kids go to private schools.	Notice we have again funded our increase in Cash Value by decreasing our 401K contribution, thus reducing our exposure to market risk.
50	Save 10% of annual income.	Defer 5% of annual income.	Save $1,500 per month.	10X your annual income, maybe more if your kids go to private schools.	
55	Save 10% of annual income.	Defer 5% of annual income.	Save $1,500 per month.	10X your annual income, maybe more if your kids go to private schools.	

continued

A Collection of Thoughts

Your Age	Savings/ Checking	Investments Tax Deferred	Investments Cash Value	Life Insurance	Rationale/ Logic
60	Save 10% of annual income.	Defer 5% of annual income.	Save $1,500 per month.	10X your annual income, maybe more if your kids go to private schools.	
65	Save 5% of annual income.	Defer 5% of annual income.	Save $1,500 per month.	5X your annual income, As you get older you can ratchet this down.	
70	Save 0% of annual income.	Defer 0% of annual income.	Save $0 per month.	None unless you happen to have younger children.	You will likely be retired at this point and will be making annual withdrawals from your portfolio.

The preceding table is intended to be a rule of thumb. These are suggestions as of the year 2017. As you get older, your situation may be different than mine. Many things could be different:

- Economic uncertainties
- Marital status
- The number of children you have
- Government tax laws
- Tax rates
- Allowable itemized tax deductions
- If you have an unusually large degree of wealth that could change your situation

Financial Goals Summary

My suggestion is to have a few simple goals:

- Life insurance: Make sure your wife and kids are taken care of financially should something happen to you. This should be anywhere from 5X to 10X your annual income.

- Savings: Make sure you have 12 months of living expenses in the bank at all times in case of an emergency.

- Investing: I think it is prudent to have a two-pronged strategy here, so below are a few rules of thumb:

  - While **Cash Value Life Insurance** is really savings, not investing, I've put it here because these two are somewhat joined at the hip when you're a young adult. Due to compound interest, you want to start saving early, but I would put money away into both a Cash Value policy and 401K. Over time, you will ratchet down the 401K and ratchet up the Cash Value policy. Your own situation, the market, and the overall economy in general will determine how quickly you make these adjustments.

  - **Maximize your company's 401K matching** if they have one. I think it is prudent to get started in a 401K when you're young, as you can afford to take on more risk when you're a young adult. For example, if they match up to 6%, then work your way towards putting in 6% of your own money. That means your 6% is really 12%. This is free money, so make sure you understand your company-sponsored benefits here.

  - As you get a little older, you'll want to ratchet down your 401K contribution while still leveraging your company's matching benefit and ratchet up your savings into a Cash Value policy. If structured properly, this enables you to "finance yourself" for bigger ticket items with your own money (cars, college expenses, home improvement projects, business opportunities, and more).

- Be flexible: As time changes, and the economy changes, and you get older, you will need to "adjust your heading" periodically.

- Financial independence: Set a goal to become financially independent by the age of 65. By age 66, hopefully, you are working because you want to, not because you have to.

A Collection of Thoughts

Life Lessons

- Get in the habit of delayed gratification.

- Keep the Rule of 72 in mind. The Rule of 72 is a quick way to determine how long it will take to double your money. For example, if you were expecting an 8% return, then it will take approximately 9 years to double your money (72/8 = 9). This rule is accurate up to about a 20% return.

- Develop the habit of automatically saving money. A rule of thumb is you should have 12 months' worth of living expenses in a liquid savings account.

- Automatically save or invest at least 10% of your monthly income for retirement, and you should be working that average up to 15%–20%.

- Aside from a house and possibly a car, don't go into debt for things that you don't need.

- Unless you are making a very large income, buy a 2- to 4-year-old car and drive it a long time. If you properly maintain your car, you should be able to drive it up to 200,000 miles. Proper maintenance involves following the manufacturer's schedule around tune-ups, oil changes, and transmission fluid flushes.

- Be cautious of investing all of your retirement money in the stock market. This is especially true as you get closer to retirement. Once you get beyond the age of 50, you'll want to begin thinking more about wealth preservation than returns.

CHAPTER

SETTING GOALS
THE BREAKFAST OF CHAMPIONS

Science fiction author Robert Heinlein once said, "In the absence of clearly defined goals, we become strangely loyal to performing daily trivia until ultimately we become enslaved by it."

This is how the average person lives. They give no thought whatsoever to developing themselves or improving their lot in life. They just don't realize it doesn't have to be that way. Show me a successful person, and I'll show you someone who is very clear about what he or she wants out of all aspects of life, and who has written plans to achieve those goals. Despite this obvious first step, less than 10 percent of people have any goals at all. Further, it is estimated that only 3 percent of people have goals that they have put in writing. Is it any wonder that the top 10 percent of people in their field make far more than the average person in the same field does? It's not an accident, luck, or a fluke.

Successful people intend to be at the top of their field, are ruthless with their time, make plans to achieve high levels of success, and, therefore, they do. It's that simple. Success is largely a choice.

Step one in attaining success, however you define it, is desire. This is very important. Inevitably strong desires produce strong results, whereas weak desires produce weak results. You have to really want something badly if you are going to put in the effort to achieve something of significance. It takes sustained effort, sometimes over a long period of time, to get what you want. But do you want to be a person of influence? Do you want to make a difference? Do you want to be in the top 3 percent of your field? The great singer/songwriter Jon Bon Jovi wrote a song that has a great line in it.

A Collection of Thoughts

"I don't want to be another wave in the ocean;
I am a rock, not just another grain of sand."

If you are not interested in making a difference, then perhaps goals aren't for you. If you are interested in being a person of consequence, then keep reading.

So, how do you leverage goal setting to turbocharge your life? Goal setting can really be broken down into just a handful of steps. Beware—be very clear that your goals are, in fact, what you want to achieve. By following the steps below, you will be on a collision course with whatever it is you desire. The famous children's author Dr. Seuss captured it this way:

"You have brains in your head. You have feet in your shoes.
You can steer yourself in any direction you choose.
You're on your own, and you know what you know.
And YOU are the one who'll decide where to go."

Goal-Setting Steps

The goal-setting process consists of five steps.

1. Decide, specifically, what it is you want.

2. Write it down and review it daily.

3. Make plans to achieve it.

4. Set a deadline for each task and each goal.

5. Take action every day toward your goal.

In pursuit of your goals, keep in mind that you're interested in progress, not perfection. If you are trying something new, you are not likely going to be very good at it at first. You are simply working to improve, to get better. As you begin to improve, it's not about being 100 percent better. It's about being 1 percent better…every day. World-renowned author Brian Tracy says, "By the yard, it's hard. But by the inch, anything is a cinch." Measure your progress in inches, not yards. Over time, the yards take care of themselves. You will be amazed at how much ground you can cover by doing something every day and by taking it in increments. A detailed plan might look something like the following.

Goal	By When?	Next Steps/Status
Goal # 1		
1. Make detailed plans in sequential priority.	May 30, 2020	
2. Goals should be in writing.	June 15, 2020	
3. Goals should be positive and in the present tense	July 30, 2020	
4. Goals should be reviewed daily.		
5. Take action, big or small, every day.		
Goal # 2		
1.		
2.		
3.		
4.		
5.		
Goal # 3		
1.		
2.		
3.		
4.		
5.		
Goal # 4		
1.		
2.		
3.		
4.		
5.		
Goal # 5		
1.		
2.		
3.		
4.		
5.		

In the business world, companies spend an enormous amount of money on research and development. I worked for EMC Corporation for a long time prior to the acquisition by Dell. EMC was a technology company that helped organizations of all sizes store, protect, manage, and analyze their information. EMC spent approximately 12 percent of annual revenues on research and development. EMC was a Fortune 160 company, generating approximately $26 billion in annual revenues prior to its acquisition. Despite its size, the Chief Executive Officer (Joe Tucci) still believed strongly that to create its future required continual investment.

The same is true of individuals. If you want to ensure you are relevant in the workplace for years to come, that requires sustained effort, a commitment to continuous learning, and you have to have a plan on how you will get better. Goals provide that plan, that road map. There are several books that I highly would recommend on the subject of goal setting:

- *Goals* by Brian Tracy
- *Think and Grow Rich* by Napoleon Hill
- *Success is a Choice* by Rick Pitino
- *Lead the Field* by Earl Nightingale (audio program)
- *The Strangest Secret* by Earl Nightingale
- *Flight Plan* by Brian Tracy
- *Focal Point* by Brian Tracy
- *You Were Born Rich* by Bob Proctor

Goal Priorities

There are a few additional points worth mentioning on this subject. The first is on the subject of priorities. It is important to set priorities; in some cases, you will make plans to achieve a goal that requires things to be done sequentially. It is obviously important to determine the most important things that need to be done.

It is also important to be clear about which activities and tasks are more important than all the others. *There is never enough time to get everything done, but there is always enough time to get the most important things done.* Knowing what the most important things are is a critical first step toward achieving anything of consequence. While this may seem like common sense, it's been my experience common sense is not always common practice.

FROM A FATHER TO A CHILD • 87

Posteriorities

Equally important is a concept called posteriorities. This is a concept I learned from Brian Tracy. A posteriority is really the opposite of a priority. A posteriority is something you must stop doing to free up time to focus on the things you should be doing. For example, you might decide you want to be the #1 salesperson for your company. One of your action plans might be to read for 30 minutes every night on the subject of selling to improve your selling skills. To free up the time to read, you might decide you need to reduce the amount of time you spend watching television. This is an example of a posteriority—something you must stop doing to make room for doing a task of higher value.

How to Write Goals

Additionally, goals should be phrased in the present tense. In other words, a written goal should be phrased in such a way *that it implies you have already achieved it.* The goal should be specific, in the present tense, and end with a deadline. For example, if you want to set a goal to lose weight, you wouldn't say, "I will lose weight." You would say, "I weigh 175 pounds by June 30, 2018. If you have an income goal, you wouldn't say, "I will make a lot of money." You would say, "I earn $150,000 by December 31, 2019." If your goal is to get better grades, you wouldn't say, "I will get better grades in school." You would say, "I earn a 3.8 grade point average by May 30, 2019."

Generally speaking, replace "I will" with *I am, I earn, I weigh, I achieve, I produce,* and so forth. You want to phrase your goals as if you have already achieved them. By phrasing your goals this way, you are convincing your subconscious mind that you have already achieved your goal. *If you believe it, you will achieve it.*

Short-term and Long-term Goals

Finally, in the short run, goals should be realistic. For example, if you've never made $100,000 in a single year in your life, setting a goal to make $1,000,000 in the upcoming year would not be realistic. There would be nothing wrong with setting a long-term goal to make $1,000,000 in a single year, but if you've never made more than $100,000 a year, then a million would not be realistic. Setting unrealistic goals can actually be counterproductive. Once you realize your unrealistic goal is out of reach, you're more likely to give up.

A Collection of Thoughts

An important point to remember is that *people tend to overestimate what they can accomplish in the next 12 months, but drastically underestimate what they can accomplish in the next 12 years*. It is very important to set realistic goals in the short run, and by short run, I mean twelve months or less. That said, dream big and think big when setting long-term goals. Set long-term goals that energize you, get you excited, and cause you to stretch. The famous retailer J.C. Penny once said, "Long-term goals keep you from being frustrated by short-term failures." Specific to long-term goals, think of the term BAG. A BAG is a Big Audacious Goal.

When setting long-term goals, such as being financially independent by the age of 50, just remember the following strategies:

- **Work Hard.** You will need to work hard over a long period of time, potentially over many years.

- **Create a Plan of Attack.** You need to have a very detailed plan of attack.
    - How much will you invest each year?
    - What skills do you need to acquire to increase your income?
    - Whose help will you need?
    - Who could you network with to gain tips and insights into how to be successful in your chosen field?
    - Where can you find the information you'll need to reach your goal?
    - How will you adjust your free time to devote the time that will be needed to achieve your goal?

- **Be flexible.** You may need to adjust or alter your plans as you acquire new skills or obtain new information. You need to be married to your goal, but not necessarily married to how you get there. Charles Darwin was a famous geologist who lived in the 1800s. Some have credited him with the following line: "It is not the strongest of the species that survive, nor the most intelligent, but the one most responsive to change." Just as a ship captain needs to alter his heading to stay on course, you may need to adjust your plans along the way.

- **Network.** You will likely need help from other people along the way. Networking with other people can help accelerate your learning curve. What others have done, you can likely do as well. It's a good practice to reach out to other successful people to learn and understand how they became successful, and then mimic what they have done. But, make sure this is a two-way street. Make time for others as well. Famous author Zig Ziglar used to say, "You will get all you want in life if you help enough other people get what they want."

I had a personal experience with this early in my career with Xerox. When I moved from Operations to Sales, I recognized I needed some help. By that time, I was a very accomplished Operations Manager, but I knew nothing about how to sell. So, what did I do? I went to a guy named Bill Dwyer. Bill was not only a successful salesperson for Xerox, but he had been consistently successful over a number of years. I'd go on sales calls, routinely make more than my fair share of mistakes, but then I'd come back to the office and ask Bill questions. Bill had a running joke with me. When I'd get back to the office, he would always ask me, "Did you sell anything?" *I loved that line.*

That was always my cue to ask him questions. Bill would always take time out of his schedule to help me and give me advice. I've never forgotten how much Bill helped me, and how gracious he was with his time. As a result, I have always made myself available to younger salespeople who needed help as my own professional career has advanced.

One thing I've noticed over the years: successful people almost always will take time to answer questions and provide advice when asked. But you have to ask. Most people won't feel bothered if you ask them for help. Rather, it is a compliment to the individual you are seeking counsel from. And, somewhere along the way, most successful people had others help them, and are generally more than willing to return the favor. I promise you every successful person had their own "Bill Dwyer" somewhere along the way.

- **Keep Score.** For long-term goals, it's important to create some milestones as you go. Keeping score will demonstrate you are making progress and will help keep you motivated.

The 10 Goal Exercise

As an action item, I would highly recommend the following exercise called The 10 Goal Exercise. This is an exercise I learned from the well-known author Brian Tracy. It works like this:

- Every morning before you go to work, take a spiral notebook and find a quiet place.

- Write down your Top 10 Goals every single day on a sheet of paper.

- The next day, rewrite the same Top 10 Goals on a new sheet of paper. Do this every day, over and over, day after day after day.

- This exercise will forge your goals into your subconscious mind. Before long, people and circumstances will begin to appear almost like magic to help you achieve your goals.

- This process of keeping your goals in front of you, continually reviewing them, will also increase your effort and activities around making them a reality.

Famous author Napoleon Hill once said, "We become what we think about most of the time." This simple exercise will draw resources, people, and circumstances to your aide beyond your wildest imagination, and help you achieve your goals far faster than you ever thought possible. As you perform this exercise over a period of weeks and months, you will be astonished at how much progress you make toward your goals. You will likely achieve more in a six-month period than you did in the previous six years. People with clear, written goals accomplish far more, far faster than people who don't have clearly defined, written goals.

Visualize Your Goals

If you really want to turbocharge this goal-writing exercise, you can add visualization to your daily routine. This exercise entails writing your goals on index cards, reading them, then closing your eyes and visualizing your goals as already achieved. The key is you need to elicit as much emotion as you possibly can while visualizing yourself as having already achieved your goal. The more emotion, the better.

The reason this is important is that your subconscious mind does not know the difference between something you have visualized repeatedly with emotion and something that has actually happened. By doing this exercise, you cement this belief into your subconscious mind with such conviction that your subconscious mind believes you are already what you are telling it you are. It then commands the body to act, perform, and achieve in congruence with what it believes to be true.

This correlation was studied by Napoleon Hill in the 1930s and is an astonishing discovery. To further cement this point, in the book *Your Infinite Power To Be Rich*, author Dr. Joseph Murphy says, "It is the belief of man that makes the difference between wealth and poverty, between success and failure, and between health and sickness. It is a cosmic law that like thoughts always produce like effects." Thus, pay special attention to the quality of your thinking. Remember:

- 80% of people don't think.
- 17% of people who think don't believe.
- The remaining 3% who *think and believe* make 97% of the money.

Albert Einstein is said to have put it another way:

"Everything is energy and that's all there is to it. Match the frequency of the reality you want, and you cannot help but get that reality. It can be no other way. This is not philosophy. This is physics."

When your habitual thinking sinks deep into your subconscious mind, your subconscious mind creates a frequency. This frequency (positive or negative) will attract the people, ideas, and circumstances to you that are congruent with what you want (positive or negative, good or bad, healthy or unhealthy). I realize this is a little deep. Some call it a Cosmic Law. Some call it tapping into the Infinite Intelligence of the Universe. Some call it Faith in God. Regardless of how you label it, science has proven this concept to be true.

Tap into this, and the world will be yours for the taking. Again, I know this is a little deep, but trust me on this. You don't have to understand how electricity works in order to be able to use it and benefit from it. The same is true here. Some of the greatest minds the world has known have tapped into this power:

- Andrew Carnegie
- Napoleon Hill
- Thomas Edison
- Albert Einstein
- Henry Ford
- Benjamin Franklin

But, *be mindful of the quality of your thoughts.* If a farmer plants corn in his field, the land will return corn. If the farmer plants weeds, the land will return weeds. The land doesn't care whether it is corn or weeds. It simply returns what is planted. The mind works the same way. If you plant positive thoughts into your subconscious mind, it will attract and return positive things. If you plant negative thoughts, it will attract and return negative things. The mind will attract and return whatever you plant.

It is a scientific fact. We become what we think about! "It can be no other way. This is not philosophy. This is physics."

Longer-Term Goals

We discussed earlier the importance of not overestimating what you can accomplish in the short term. But for longer-term goals, throw logic, conventional wisdom, assumptions, and artificial boundaries out the window. When setting long-term goals, don't think *evolutionary*, think *revolutionary*. Boundaries are artificial, not hard ceilings. And because boundaries are artificial, they can be altered. Rather than allowing yourself to be constrained by what you think is possible, think "impossible" instead. *Focus on possibilities rather than constraints. Don't limit your long-term goals to what you think you can achieve. This is the single biggest mistake people make when setting long-term goals.*

According to Bob Proctor, famous author and success coach, "Most people are not going after what they want. Even some of the most serious goal seekers and goal setters, they are going after what they think they can get." Big difference.

A great example of this comes from our 35th President, John F. Kennedy. In the late 1950s/early 1960s, a cold war had begun between the United States and the Soviet Union. At that time, we were behind the Soviets in terms of space exploration. President Kennedy decided to address Congress on what he called matters of Urgent National Needs on May 25, 1961. Essentially he was going to Congress to ask for an additional $7 to $9 billion for NASA to ramp up our space program. At that time, this was an unheard of, almost controversial, amount of money. Below is an excerpt from his speech.

"I believe that this nation should commit itself to achieving the goal, before this decade is out, of landing a man on the moon and returning him safely to the earth. No single space project in this period will be more impressive to mankind, or more important for the long-range exploration of space."

– John F. Kennedy

This long-term goal President Kennedy stated is worth a few comments:

- At the time of this speech, the technology to get to the moon, much less land on it, had not been invented or developed. Yet, that didn't stop President Kennedy from stating the goal anyway.
- Note the goal he states is very specific.
- He put the goal in writing.
- He set a deadline.
- He presented a grand vision, one that inspired an entire nation.

This speech contained the very aspects of long-term goal setting that we've discussed in this chapter. The United States did, in fact, land on the moon on July 20, 1969, a full eight years after President Kennedy set the goal. This is a classic, historically significant example of long-term goal setting, and how effective it can be.

To bring this closer to home, let's say a long-term goal for you is you want to be a millionaire by the age of 40. You don't have to have all the answers on how you will achieve that goal at the time you set the goal. You simply have to have the specific goal, write it down, visualize yourself as a millionaire, affirm that goal day-after-day to implant it into your sub-conscious mind, and the answers will begin to appear over time. While visualizing this goal, see yourself as a millionaire. What clothes would you be wearing? What kind of car would you be driving? What kind of house would you be living in? How much money would you see in your monthly bank statement? How much would you be able to give to various charities of your choice?

Visualize these things with emotion, and once you've convinced your subconscious mind that you are a millionaire, the people, circumstances, and solutions will begin to appear to help you achieve this goal. This is a scientific fact. Then, as these ideas and circumstances begin to appear, you *must* take action!

Create a Bucket List

The following story also illustrates how impactful goals can be. One of the more exciting things you can do in life is to put together a bucket list. A bucket list is a list of everything you would like to have, be, or do in your lifetime. In this exercise, don't limit yourself with preconceived notions on what you can accomplish or what you think is possible for you. Set big, audacious goals. The bigger the goals, the better, as this individual eventually found out. Chris Chickering, psychotherapist and recording artist, wrote the following regarding long-term goals.

The Crazy Crazy Ones

Over 20 years ago, when I was in college, I created a bucket list. At the very top of that list, I wrote down the words: I want to become a recording artist. And I have to be honest, when I wrote it, I thought that goal was nearly impossible for me to achieve. I could crank out a good Rolling Stones cover on my guitar and could rock the house at parties, but didn't have the first clue about how to write a song, let alone one that might eventually make it on the radio…but I wrote it down anyway because I decided to believe some crazy guy I'd heard at a seminar shouting about how you HAVE TO create a bucket list and fill it with grand visions, and how *people that write their goals down achieve them 97% of the time.*

As the years rolled by, I was able to knock a number of dreams off the list, but that one dream I really wanted – *my crazy recording artist dream* remained an impossible enigma. Until one day, about 7 years ago, when I finally realized something about myself:

The reason I kept putting off my #1 dream was I had been carrying around some major self-limiting beliefs in regards to my ability to pull it off including:

• You aren't talented enough.

• It will fail eventually, so why try?

• They'll find you are a fraud eventually.

• You don't deserve it.

• You really don't want that anyway.

And in that moment of self-awareness, a strange thing happened: the part of me that believed I could do it – that part of me that wrote the dream down in the first place – finally won over and I made the decision to take the first step by producing one of my songs: *Stay.*

Since that point, 50 songs, two albums and a website later, I have learned that what seems so scary and "impossible," really isn't so. The key is to just take the first step and never stop taking those steps, ever, and to realize – if you have been putting off one of your dreams or are trying to forget you even had one! – Then there is a good chance you might be carrying around some false self-limiting beliefs and programming too.

So take a little time to look inside and see what's going on in your head. Why have you put off your dream? Why has your dream stalled? Instead of listening to the surface excuses, get quiet and listen deeper to the self-limiting beliefs that might reside within you…and bring those to the surface. Think about your dream, then try my self-limiting beliefs above on for size and see how they fit. Painful, isn't it?

I empathize: achieving your dreams is not easy, but guess what: You can start. You can start right now manifesting your crazy dream, today. There is still nothing stopping you, and so I'm going to encourage you right now to take the first step towards your "impossible" dream, and never stop taking those steps, *ever*.

That's the decision I made, and today I am accomplishing things I never thought possible, including hearing my songs on the radio all because I finally made the decision to step outside my comfort zone and take action!

So, if you're sick and tired of putting your dream off, here's some heart-felt advice:

1. #1 – Take action. You may stumble. You may fall, you might even go backwards, but keep going. You will learn along the way and eventually succeed.

2. To avoid getting overwhelmed, break down your "to do" list into extremely small tasks, and be sure to pat yourself on the back for every single task you complete. Don't expect anyone else to pat you on the back. If they do great, but do not let this impact how you feel one way or the other. Your emotions are determined by how you think about what you are doing.

3. Ideally (but not totally necessary) find a mentor who has successfully done it before. It will make your journey smoother.

4. Create or revamp a bucket list and fill it with GRAND visions and dreams.

5. Wake up every day and make some progress towards your dream every day.

6. Make "do it now" your mantra. Do not put off for tomorrow what can be done right now.

7. Surround yourself with people who believe in your dreams, and people who are doing the same in their life.

8. Realize: success is a marathon not a sprint.

9. To get your internal game where it needs to be, create positive mantras, write them down, make them your screen saver and paste them on your bathroom mirror. Don't know what to write? Try these on for size:

   – I deserve it and am destined to achieve greatness as long as I put the work in.

   – I am an unstoppable force for good.

   – The only failure is giving up.

   – The joy is in the journey.

I sincerely hope you take the first step now towards your dream. You will not regret it, I promise, and know this: when you take steps towards your dream and your higher-self, you are doing a great service to the world and everyone around you, because guess what? Everyone has fear and self-doubt about achieving their grandest desires, so when you move towards your crazy-dream, you show others by example that their crazy-dream is possible to achieve as well.

To the greatness within,

Chris Chickering

How Goals Are Vital

The real truth most people fail to recognize is they can have, be, or do anything they really want in life, so long as they are willing to work for it. Anything someone else has achieved, within reason, you can likely do as well. Goals can help you in three areas that are vital to achievement in any endeavor: **direction**, **hard work**, and **determination**.

Direction

Success requires a clear direction, much like the rudder of a ship. Without a rudder, a ship would veer aimlessly in one direction or the other, moving in whatever direction the currents or wind took them. But the rudder guides the ship in the direction the captain wants it to go. Goals work the same way in your life. A goal will provide you the direction, the roadmap, to guide you in what choices you make, how you spend your time, and how you prioritize your day-to-day activities.

For example, if you want to be the number one sales representative in your organization, you might start to work backward from that goal. The list below is in reverse order:

1. Be the number one sales representative in the organization, as measured by revenue produced. Remember to be specific, so this might instead say, "I produce $10 million in revenue for XYZ Corporation in 2018."

2. Produce a large number of proposals. Be specific, so this might say, "I write one proposal per week."

3. Meet face to face with 12 clients per week.

4. Make 50 phone calls per day in order to meet with 12 clients per week.

Now, you might determine that in order to meet with 12 clients per week, you need to be working on proposals after hours or on weekends. This will require a choice. Do you watch TV for several hours each night at home, or do you carve out an hour or two to work on your proposals, knowing this will enable you to spend more time in front of your clients during the business day.

Without knowing exactly, in very specific terms, what you need to accomplish, and in what time frame, it is very easy to let life knock you off course. Goals will help drive your activities because you will be very clear about what you are trying to accomplish and will have a plan to achieve it.

Hard Work

Goal achievement will likely require long hours of hard work, sustained over a period of time. Achieving worthwhile things in life is rarely easy. For every person that has won the lottery, I'll show you one hundred million people who are struggling through life. *Big Goals require Big Effort.* Winning the lottery may be easy, but it is not a strategy, and not likely to happen for the vast majority of people. The odds are simply not in your favor. *If you want to put the odds in your favor, the single greatest equalizer is hard work.*

In Chapter 1, I mentioned Pete Rose, the all-time hits leader in Major League Baseball. "Charlie Hustle" was notorious for a second-to-none work ethic, and for always giving it 110% when he played. A by-product of his work ethic was consistency. Pete Rose's batting average over his 24-year career was an impressive .303. But in addition, he was exceptionally consistent. He had a run in the prime of his career (1965–1981) where he hit over .300 in 15 of 17 years—remarkable! Many would argue Ted Williams was the greatest hitter of all time. Perhaps Mickey Mantle was the most versatile hitter of all time, in that he hit with both power and average. Hank Aaron or Babe Ruth, one could argue, were the greatest home run hitters of all time. But Rose had to be the most consistent hitter of all time. Why? Because he had, arguably, the most consistent work habits of all time. *Consistent work habits produce consistent results.* It's really no more complicated than that.

For example, let's return to my sales representative scenario. Obviously, people that are achieving high levels of success are intelligent, highly skilled people. That said, I want to illustrate a point regarding how hard work is an equalizer to achievement. Let's say Sales Representative A is highly skilled and wins 9 out of every 10 deals he is involved in. Sales Representative B is not that skilled and only wins 1 out of every 10 deals she is involved in. Now the question: is it possible for Sales Representative B to out-produce Sales Representative A? The answer is absolutely!

Let's say Sales Representative B works extraordinarily hard and competes in 100 deals. Over the same time frame, Sales Representative A has become complacent, using his skill to achieve his quota. As a result, Sales Representative A only competes in 10 deals. Using the winning ratios mentioned above, their respective results are as follows:

- Sales Representative A: 10 attempts x 90% batting average = 9 wins
- Sales Representative B: 100 attempts x 10% batting average = 10 wins

Plain old-fashioned hard work can mask a lot of other issues. And you have complete control over how hard you decide to work. As I'm writing this book, I've been in sales for approaching twenty years. I can tell you no sales manager I have ever worked for kept track of how many deals I lost. What is tracked, and tracked very closely, is how many times you win. In my example above, Sales Representative B out-sold and out-produced Sales Representative A...not through skill, but through persistent hard work.

Determination

And finally, achieving big goals requires dogged, persistent determination. You can't give up when you have a setback, or if things are not going exactly as you planned. This is precisely what most people do. They give up, or quit, without realizing how close they may be to achieving their goal. Having clearly defined written goals makes it less likely you will quit when the going gets tough. The very act of putting goals in writing puts teeth into your goal and helps galvanize your attitude toward them.

The famous author Napoleon Hill once said for every failure, there is an equal or greater benefit just around the corner, so long as you don't give up. Everyone fails from time to time. Determined people ensure that they learn from failure or mistakes. This learning process enables them to fail forward. Failing forward is about making sure you learn a lesson from each and every setback.

"All parents believe their children can do the impossible.
They thought it the minute we were born, and no matter how hard
we've tried to prove them wrong, they all think it about us now.
And the really annoying thing is, they're probably right."

Cathy Guisewite, Cartoonist

Life Lessons

• Never get in the way of a boy and his dreams.

• If it's worth having, it's worth working for.

• Dream Big, Think Big.

• Always be working on well-thought-out, written goals.

• Take time to think and plan.

• Practice the Top 10 Goals Exercise daily.

CHAPTER

ACCOUNTABILITY AND RESPONSIBILITY

DANCE TO YOUR OWN BEAT

As I've gotten older, I've noticed one quality that seems to be pervasively missing in society today. That quality is accountability. We now live in a "what's in it for me" society, where people expect things for nothing. They also frequently expect things instantaneously, something Hall of Fame basketball coach Rick Pitino calls the "microwave society."

Our government has not helped here, in that there are more government handouts and programs than we as a nation can afford. An unintended consequence of this is we make people dependent on the government. One example of this is food stamps, which increased significantly under President Barack Obama. Food stamps for the poor is a noble cause. That said, during his time in office (2009–2017), food stamp recipients increased by three-fold. Now, are there three times as many people going hungry today than there were when he took office in 2009? I don't think so. We have systematically reduced the requirements to obtain food stamps, and we've allowed people to receive this benefit far longer than they used to.

Now, I'm not opposed to safety nets for people who legitimately need help. The fact is that sometimes people do need a helping hand. However, we need to be careful here. Providing too many government-sponsored programs for too long provides a disincentive to work. That isn't good for anybody. Stephen Covey once said, *"Give a man a fish, you feed him for a day. Teach a man how to fish, and you feed him for a lifetime."*

A Collection of Thoughts

There is nothing wrong with giving people a hand for a finite period of time as a safety net. *But, we should be teaching people how to fish, not giving them fish indefinitely.* Making people dependent on government programs hurts the very people they are intended to help, in that it contributes to them being a permanent member of the underclass.

Accountability and Responsibility

Regarding the subject of accountability and responsibility, there are several things that come to mind here:

- Be able to be counted on to do what you say you're going to do
- Be a person that doesn't make excuses
- Have the courage to take responsibility for outcomes, good or bad, rather than blaming others
- Have the courage to do what is right, even in the face of ridicule, rather than doing what is popular
- Be accountable and responsible in your home life

Let's dive into each one of these areas in more detail.

Be a Person Who Can Be Counted on to Do What You Say

Doing what you say you're going to do, following through, seems to have gone out of style just like plaid pants or pastel ties. Many people will simply do what is easy or expedient, regardless of what they said they would do or how it impacts others. While doing what you say isn't always easy, it is a sure-fire way to develop a sterling reputation. This is true both personally and professionally.

Professionally speaking, if you consistently do what you say you're going to do, you will begin to notice greater levels of responsibility come your way. Leaders are people who don't make decisions based on popularity or expediency. And they always follow through. This type of consistency and dependability is, to a large extent, how they rose within their respective organizations in the first place.

Senior management within any organization tends to promote people based on four key attributes:

- Producing results
- Being able to get along with people (peers, co-workers, and clients alike)

- Being able to be counted on
- Being efficient in getting things done

Whether we are talking about getting a report in on time, delivering a sales forecast, or completing a project on time and/or under budget, one way to endear yourself to your superiors is to develop a reputation that goes something like the following: "If Nicholas says it's going to happen, then you can take it to the bank."

Back in the early 1990s, I was a member of a management team with Xerox Business Services. We had a few reports that had to be turned in every Monday morning to our General Manager (GM) regarding the activities of the previous week. I can remember our GM getting very irritated when someone didn't turn all of his reports in on time. He would often say, "If you aren't on top of your paperwork, then that makes me wonder what else are you not on top of?" As I have moved into various leadership positions, I have found that is a pretty good barometer.

From a personal standpoint, doing what you say is equally important. For example, let's say you tell your son you will throw the ball with him when you get home from work. But when you get home, you decide to respond to emails or take a phone call and run out of time to play with your son. What does that say to your son? What your son hears you say by your actions is, "My dad has other things to do that are more important than I am." It doesn't matter how many times you tell your son you love him and that he is important to you. If your actions consistently lead him to believe there are other things more important than him, that is what he will hear and believe.

Additionally, you are teaching your kids things by your mere actions. If you can't be counted on to do what you say you will do, you are indirectly teaching your kids it's OK to not keep your word. The lesson we should be teaching our kids, and reinforcing at every opportunity, is that it is not OK to say one thing and do another. If kids, sons and daughters alike, learned to always do what they say they are going to do, then our country, and society as a whole, would be much better off.

Be a Person Who Doesn't Make Excuses

How many people do you know, or have you come across, who are never at fault? If something goes wrong in their life, personally or professionally, it's never their fault. When you cross paths with a person like this, how do you feel about them? Are they the type of person you enjoy hanging out with? People who make excuses suffer from a disease I like to call "excusitis". My guess is these are people you avoid like the plague. So, don't be one of them. The Golden Rule applies here. If you don't like people who make excuses, then don't be a person that makes excuses. Or to borrow a phrase from a grade schooler as an example of what not to do, "My dog ate my homework." This excuse sounds, and is, ridiculous. Yet many adults use essentially the same excuse all the time. You will find it is liberating to be able to accept responsibility, to not make excuses.

Circumstances are not inherent personal traits and are not permanent. Therefore, through effort and planning, circumstances can be changed over time. If something in your life goes wrong, get in the habit of blaming yourself first. Then, go about making new plans to achieve whatever it is you are trying to accomplish.

I mentioned Coach Huse earlier, a high school basketball coach in Brownsburg, Indiana. I was playing basketball for Coach Huse in a summer league when I was 14 years old. Our team was getting beat, and I was getting frustrated with a few of my team mates who were taking quick, poor shots. I was the leading scorer and had gone the entire first quarter without getting a single shot off. At the end of the first quarter, I was walking toward the bench, muttering (complaining really) to myself how unhappy I was with my team mates. Coach Huse overheard me and lit into me like only my dad would. He yelled at me the entire time out. I don't recall everything he said, but the one thing I've never forgotten was this, "If you don't like what's going on, then do something about it. Change it. Don't complain about it!"

What a great lesson. He chewed me out over 30 years ago, and I can still hear those words ringing in my ears. You have the ability to change circumstances, so don't waste time complaining about them. Generally speaking nobody cares about your problems anyway. Rather than complain about problems, or blame someone else for them, simply get busy fixing them.

A famous Hall of Fame football coach named Bill Parcells is a good example of a guy that doesn't make excuses. He was coaching the Dallas Cowboys late in his career, and he rebuilt a terrible team very quickly. In his fourth season, they had made the playoffs. They were playing in the 2006 NFC Wild Card game in Seattle and could have won the game except for a botched field goal attempt. They were down 21 to 20 with 1:16 minutes left in the game. The holder, quarterback Tony Romo, fumbled the snap, and they were not able to convert the field goal. As you can imagine, reporters fixated on this one play. Coach Parcells took a different approach. Rather than dwell on one play, or one player, he simply said had they executed better on both sides of the ball the game would not have come down to that one play. He had a line I've always remembered, "You are what your record says you are." Their record that year was 9 wins 7 losses. What a way to diffuse a situation for a player, in this case Tony Romo.

Coach Bob Knight is another example of a terrific leader. In 1984, Coach Knight took a very young Indiana University team into the NCAA tournament. Because they were young, many people didn't expect them to go very far. In the third round of the tournament, they upset North Carolina, who was the #1 team in the country led by Michael Jordan (I know you've heard of him). With this win, Indiana advanced to the Elite 8, one game away from a trip to the Final Four.

Indiana's leading scorer that year was a freshman named Steve Alford. Alford scored 27 points in the win over North Carolina. Indiana faced Virginia in the next round, and they obviously decided to focus on stopping Alford, which they did. They held him to 6 points. After the game, Coach Knight was asked why Alford had a bad game. He took the blame for Indiana's loss, while also crediting Virginia. He said, and I'm paraphrasing, "Alford didn't have a bad game. I didn't adequately prepare him for the Virginia game." What a great leader.

Have the Courage to Take Responsibility Rather than Blaming Others

Blaming others first is an attitude that rears its ugly head in politics as well as in the workplace. People who blame others for their failures may get away with it in the short run, but people will not follow someone like this for any length of time.

One of our country's leaders, our 35th president, John F. Kennedy, practiced this attitude during the infamous Bay of Pigs incident. When President Kennedy took office in January 1961, he inherited an operation from the CIA to overthrow the leader of Cuba, a man named Fidel Castro. At that time, the United States was very concerned about the spread of communism, and Cuba was a communist country. Given Cuba is 90 miles south of the tip of Florida, conventional wisdom said Castro had to go.

The CIA helped train 1,300 exiled Cuban military personnel who wanted to overthrow the Cuban government. These militants were trained in guerilla warfare, sabotage, and infiltration. The plan was for these militants to attack the Bay of Pigs, Cuba. Additionally, the CIA promised to provide cover by air and sea to help them. After the initial attack, there was a planned Phase 2 airstrike for additional bombing of Cuban military targets. The idea was as this brigade picked up steam, a counter-revolutionary movement would be started, and mass military defections would result. As this movement picked up steam, a nationwide chain reaction would ultimately cause the entire Castro regime to collapse.

The invasion began on April 17, 1961. After four days, 89 of these men had been killed, and the remainder were taken prisoners. What happened? Upon learning the invasion was not going well, President Kennedy called off the second strategic airstrike, in that the US didn't want to be linked directly to the operation for fear of retaliation by the Soviet Union (a Castro backer).

While privately, President Kennedy fumed, feeling the CIA had misled him on the operation in general. The CIA had assured Kennedy that the operation would be a lay-up, or relatively easy; obviously, that didn't turn out to be the case. However, publicly he calmly took full responsibility for the botched invasion. He noted in an exchange with the media, "There's an old saying that victory has a hundred fathers and defeat is an orphan…I'm the responsible officer of the government…" He was saying essentially that as Commander-in-Chief, it was his responsibility. It would have been easy for President Kennedy to blame the entire episode on the CIA, who came up with and planned the entire invasion. In fact, the planning and initial approval occurred during the Eisenhower Administration. That said, the botched invasion occurred on his watch, and he took full responsibility for it.

After taking full responsibility, an interesting thing happened. President Kennedy's approval ratings soared. The point here is people respect someone who is not afraid to shoulder more than their fair share of the blame, and then go about resolving a situation or problem.

Be a Person Who Does What Is Right, Not What Is Popular

You will no doubt face choices in life where nobody will really know what you did. This is precisely when character counts the most. Many people will do what is right when they know they will get caught for doing the wrong thing. A person of high character does the right thing simply because they will know what they did.

A Collection of Thoughts

If you find yourself in a position where you have to spin a story to explain or justify your actions, then you likely aren't doing the right thing. Another way to look at this is if you are faced with a difficult decision, imagine your actions appearing on the front page of the newspaper. If this wouldn't bother you, go ahead and do it. If you would be embarrassed for others to find out what you did, then it is probably not something you should be doing.

I'll reference another US President for this topic. President Ronald Reagan was elected in 1980 as our 40th President. President Reagan came into office focused on two things:

- Winning the Cold War with the Soviet Union
- Reigniting our sluggish economy

Specific to the Soviet Union, the US had had a policy dating back to the 1950s to halt the spread of communism in the world. This standoff between the United States and the Soviet Union became known as the Cold War. No shots were fired, no missiles were launched, war was not waged, but it would be fair to say it was a long, protracted war along ideological lines.

Fast forward to the 1980s. President Reagan was determined to win the Cold War, as he was very concerned about the spread of communism. His foreign policy came to be known as the Reagan Doctrine. The Reagan Doctrine essentially said this:

- Eliminate or marginalize Soviet Union influence across the globe
- Provide overt and covert support to anti-communist countries and movements to prevent the spread of communism
- Replace communist-influenced governments with governments based on democracies in Africa, Asia, and Latin America

The Reagan Doctrine only lasted about a decade, in full effect until the fall of the Soviet Union in 1991.

President Reagan was negotiating with the President of the Soviet Union, Mikhail Gorbachev, regarding a Nuclear Missile Treaty in October 1986. As a part of their negotiations, the Soviet Union wanted President Reagan to stop the development of our "Star Wars" initiative. At a high level, this technology was comprised of space-based satellites that could shoot incoming nuclear missiles out of the sky before they reached the US. With this type of sophisticated missile defense system, it would largely make offensive weaponry obsolete. The Soviet Union was highly concerned about

A Collection of Thoughts

this technology, as it would swing the balance of power toward the US. The formal name for this program was the Strategic Defense Initiative (SDI). President Reagan had made it clear from the outset of the negotiations that SDI was not negotiable. The US would fervently pursue this missile defense system with or without a treaty with the USSR.

After days of negotiating, the US and the Soviet Union were relatively close to a deal that would reduce the inventory of nuclear missiles that both countries had. Toward the end of another long day of negotiations, the Soviet Leader again brought up their insistence that the US must stop the development of SDI before the Soviets would sign a Nuclear Missile Treaty. Upon hearing this, President Reagan is said to have gotten up and walked out of the negotiations. He was largely criticized for this, given the two sides were nearing a historic peace treaty. The US press widely criticized Reagan, many suggesting that he was a warmonger. While unpopular to many, President Reagan stuck to his guns, saying essentially that no deal is better than a bad one. He went on to say SDI enabled the US to negotiate from a position of strength and that SDI made the US and our allies abroad, more safe, not less safe. SDI, under no circumstances, was negotiable.

As it turned out, President Reagan ended up being right. He felt the economy of the Soviet Union was in shambles, and that the US had more leverage than many believed in nuclear negotiations. Ultimately, the Soviet Union came back to the negotiations table a year later, and the Intermediate-Range Nuclear Forces (INF) Treaty was signed in 1987 that, for the first time, eliminated an entire category of nuclear weapons. And true to his word, we continued to develop SDI.

The moral of the story is that if you firmly believe you are right, then stick to your guns (no pun intended). Stick to your guns even if it's an unpopular position.

Be Accountable and Responsible in Your Home Life

Here are a few other topics that are worthy of a quick discussion, as they continue this chapter's theme of accountability and responsibility: raising kids, giving to charity, taking care of your home, and going to church every Sunday.

Raising Kids

I think the first time I really began to understand what true love was involved my engagement to my wife, Wendi. I realized true love is when you are willing to put someone else's needs before your own. During my single days, I dated several gals that were attractive, nice, bright, and fun. But it wasn't until I met Wendi that I was truly prepared to put another person's wants and needs before my own. I think the same thing applies to children. Without a doubt, there will be demands placed on you that have to be addressed from a career standpoint, such as travel, long hours, and more. After all, as a parent, our first responsibility to our children is food, shelter, and clothing. But when it comes to children, it's important to remember love is a four-letter word to them, and that word is spelled T-I-M-E.

At an early age, children don't understand the reasons why their parents get called away. While many times as parents, we will have to miss events in our children's lives that are unavoidable, *we need to remember children will equate how much time you spend with them with how much you love them.* Thus, attending Little League games, soccer tournaments, parent/teacher conferences, and school recitals are a language children understand far more than the words "I love you." My advice here is simple. If you aren't willing to be a responsible parent and put your kids first, then don't have them in the first place.

Growing up, I played sports year-round. As a youth, I played basketball, flag football, tackle football, baseball, floor hockey, tennis, and golf. In some instances, I played in more than one league at the same time. When I was in the sixth grade, I played in three different basketball leagues in a single year. As I got into junior high school, I narrowed my focus to basketball, football, and baseball. My guess is that in any given year, I participated in roughly 70 to 80 organized games per year, as there were always summer leagues for both basketball and baseball in addition to playing for my school.

From the time I was five years old until the day I graduated from high school, my best guess is I played in approximately 1,000 organized games over 13 years. Keep in mind that this was before travel ball and AAU tournaments. At that time, this was a lot of games. Without hesitation, I can guarantee you I can count on both hands the number of games my parents missed. I had friends whose mom or dad only came occasionally, or only came when it was convenient. I never told my parents how much that meant to me, but I remember thinking at the time it was pretty neat they were always there. It was readily apparent they took a sincere, genuine interest in what I was doing. While my parents told me they loved me frequently growing up, it was the amount of time they spent following me around that spoke volumes of how much they cared for me. Their actions spoke louder than their words.

Upon deciding to have children, my wife and I made a decision that we felt it was important that one of us stay at home to raise our kids during their formative years, with ultimately that privilege falling on my wife. While I don't mean to criticize parents who both work, as in many cases, both parents need to work to satisfy the essentials for their children: food, shelter, and clothing. However, I also believe many parents both work so they can drive the Lexus instead of the Chevy, or live in a 5,000 square foot house instead of a 3,000 square foot house, or belong to a well-respected country club instead of the local YMCA.

Now, make no mistake about it. I like the finer things in life too. However, my wife and I have gotten into the habit of practicing delayed gratification. While we have been fortunate to be able to afford many things on that list yet still have one of us stay at home, we have not done so at the expense of our children. In my opinion, there will never be a greater honor, privilege, or responsibility than performing well as a parent. My mom recently passed on the following poem. As I wrote this chapter I was in my late forties, and she is still very much my mom!

If I Had a Boy
By Frank Carleton Nelson

If I had a boy, I would say to him: "Son,
Be fair and be square in the race you must run,
Be brave if you lose and be meek if you win,
Be better and nobler than I've ever been,
Be honest and fearless in all that you do
And honor the name I have given to you."

If I had a boy, I would want him to know
We reap in this life just about as much as we sow,
And we get what we earn, be it little or great,
Regardless of luck and regardless of fate.
I would teach him and show him, the best that I could,
That it pays to be honest and upright and good.

I would make him a pal and partner of mine,
And show him the things in this world that are fine.
I would show him the things that are wicked and bad,
For I figure this knowledge should come from his dad, too
And to all of my promises strive to be true.

We would grow up together and I'd be a boy
And share in his trouble and share in his joy.
We would work out problems together and then
We would lay out our plans when we both would be men.
And oh, what a wonderful joy it would be!
No pleasure in life could be greater to me.

Giving to Charity

While it's obviously a personal decision, you should give to charities that are important to you to the extent you can afford. John F. Kennedy once said, "For of those to whom much is given much is required." There are many people that will be less fortunate than you, and if you can afford to give, I think you should.

The church talks about time and treasure. If you find you don't have a lot of disposable income to donate, then you might consider donating your time. A few examples include joining the church choir or volunteering to help maintain the grounds of a not-for-profit organization.

Regarding treasure, a good rule of thumb is to give 5 percent of your income to charities. Again, make sure you aren't sacrificing your ability to provide food, shelter, and clothing to your family. But once those things are covered, consider giving 5 percent to a charity or various charities. As an example, you could set aside 5 percent of your monthly income into a separate savings account automatically. Once you get into this habit, it's not likely you will miss 5 percent. Throughout the course of the year, you can pull money from this charity account and give it to worthy charities of your choice. They will appreciate it, and so will you. As the Bible says, "It is in giving that we receive."

Taking Care of your Home

The single greatest investment you will ever make is your home. Therefore, you will want to maintain it. Keeping up with routine maintenance, such as painting, cleaning carpets, and repairing normal wear and tear, should be addressed on a regular basis.

You'll also want to take care of the exterior of the home, which includes your lawn and landscaping. A good rule of thumb is clean and green. Fertilizing in the spring and fall, and keeping the lawn watered throughout the summer months will keep your lawn in good shape. Additionally, you should keep your shrubs and bushes trimmed. Successful people keep the exterior of their homes looking their best at all times. This maintains the value of your home. It also produces goodwill with your neighbors. People don't like to live next to people whose yard is a mess.

It's been said your outer world is a reflection of your inner world. If your home is in disrepair, or disorganized, what are you telling and showing others about yourself? I once read a story a number of years ago where a father was reading the newspaper. His little boy was playing on the floor and was a little bored. "Daddy, I'm bored," said the little boy. So, the father took a picture of a house from the newspaper, tore it up into pieces, and told his little boy to put it back together. To the Father's surprise, the little boy had put this puzzle together in no time. The father was amazed and asked him, "How did you put the puzzle together so fast?" The little boy replied, "There was a picture of a man on the back. I put the man together, and then the house was back together too." The father replied, "That's right, son. When a man is together on the inside, his outer world is together too."

Going to Church Every Sunday

God gave us the week, so the least we can do is give him an hour on Sunday. This is sound advice from my mom. Some people are rather public with their faith. I'm not saying there is anything wrong with that, as people should practice their faith in a way that is comfortable for them. Personally, I tend to be pretty private, but my faith is definitely a big part of my life. My hope for you is that it becomes a big part of your life too. Faith can be a calming presence when times are tough.

Life Lessons

- Always do what you say you're going to do.
- Never make excuses. Successful people spend their time producing results, not producing excuses.
- Take responsibility for your actions: your successes and your failures.
- Never blame others for your circumstance in life, for you have the ability to change circumstances.
- Go to church every Sunday. "God gave you the week. The least you can do is give him an hour." - Judy Johns (my mom)

CHAPTER

6

CRITICAL SUCCESS FACTORS
DARE TO BE GREAT

Successful people do many things well. But one area where they are really good is they are highly effective strategic thinkers. They think through what needs to be done and in what order things need to be completed. One thing specific to good time management is you will never have enough time to do everything, but you always have enough time to do what is most important.

You've no doubt heard of the 80/20 rule. This principle was first observed by an economist named Vifredo Pareto. In 1906 he observed that in Italy, 20% of the population owned 80% of the land. Upon further study, he also observed that 20% of the pea pods in his garden produced 80% of the peas. As he continued to study this phenomenon, this rule of thumb continued to hold true, whether it was landowners, pea pods, or employee productivity. Thus, the Pareto Principle was formed. This rule can apply to virtually anything:

- 20% of what you do determines 80% of the results you get.
- The top 20% of salespeople produce 80% of the revenue for a company.
- The top 20% of income earners make as much as the bottom 80%.
- The top 20% of a company's clients will produce 80% of their revenues.
- The top 20% of your investments will produce 80% of your returns.
- The top 20% of taxpayers pay 80% of the tax burden.
- And so on...

A Collection of Thoughts

A good exercise is to apply the 80/20 rule to everything you do: your personal life, relationships, investments, exercise, diet, hobbies, your career, …everything. That said, there is no area of your life that the 80/20 rule can help provide more leverage and efficiency to your efforts than your professional career.

Once you've chosen your professional field, you will need to determine how to be successful. This success will entail becoming very good at a few things. It is better to know a lot about a few things than to know a little about a lot of things. The world will pay you handsomely if you are an expert at what you do. There is an old saying, "The fox that chases two rabbits captures neither." This is true in life also.

Characteristics of Successful People

The remainder of this chapter will explore five characteristics that all successful people have:

(1) Positive attitude

(2) Extraordinary work ethic

(3) Lifelong commitment to continuous learning

(4) Exceptional at managing their time

(5) Take time to think

(1) Positive Attitude

As you go through life, you will encounter ups and downs, good times and bad. It's been said life isn't about what happens; it's more about how you react to what happens. One very important point: nobody can control your thoughts. Nobody can control how you feel about yourself. Nobody can control what goes on between your ears. There will always be things that occur that are completely out of your control. But you always have complete control of your mind and your attitude.

I would submit to you it is impossible to hold a positive and negative thought in your mind at the same time. By focusing on maintaining a positive attitude, you will simultaneously eliminate negative thoughts from entering your mind. Similar to how a thick, green lawn crowds out weeds from growing, positive thoughts crowd out negative thoughts from taking root.

Now, what is a positive thought? Sounds like a simple enough question. Is it feeling good? Is it being happy on a sunny day? Not quite. Positive thoughts are more specific than that. A few examples:

- Reviewing your goals, both verbally and written, every day
- Telling yourself, *I can, I will, I have, I achieve*
- Focusing on helping others achieve their goals

Let's say you are playing a basketball game with some friends, and on this particular day, you are not playing well. If you get extremely upset about your own play, several things happen. First, you take the fun out of the game for everyone else. Nobody wants to play with someone who has a bad attitude. Second, don't ever let a bad game, or a bad play, cause you to have a bad attitude. *In the history of mankind, no one has accomplished anything with a negative attitude.* If you make a bad play, and that consumes your mind and your thinking, are you more likely or less likely to make "another bad play? The answer is obvious; you are more likely to make another bad play if that is what is consuming your thinking. Conversely, if you are expecting to make a good play, you are far more likely to make a good play the next time. And finally, a bad attitude causes negative thoughts to fill your mind. Nothing good has ever come from a mind filled with negative thoughts.

Staying positive, focusing on your goals, and expecting/believing good things will happen is one of the best ways to be happy. Elvis Presley, arguably one of the greatest, most charismatic, most versatile entertainers of all time, once defined happiness as follows: "Happiness is having someone to love, something to look forward to, and something to do." Well said.

One final thought on attitude comes from a poem written by Charles R. Swindoll. By the way, my dad gave this to me.

Attitude

The longer I live, the more I realize the impact of attitude on life.

Attitude, to me, is more important than facts.
It is more important than the past,

than education, than money, than circumstance, than failures,
than successes, than what other people think or say or do.

It is more important than appearance, giftedness or skill.

It will make or break a company…a church…a home.

The remarkable thing is we have a choice everyday regarding the attitude we will embrace for that day. We cannot change our past…

A Collection of Thoughts

We cannot change the fact that people will act in a certain way.

We cannot change the inevitable.
The only thing we can do is play on the one

string we have, and that is our attitude!

I am convinced that life is 10% what happens to me and
90% how I react to it. And so it is with you…

We are in charge of our attitudes!

(2) Extraordinary Work Ethic

There are two ways to accomplish significant things. One is to develop a skill set that is well above average. Another approach is to get in the habit of outworking everyone in sight. Get up a little earlier, stay a little later, do more than what is required, expect more of yourself than any potential manager could possibly expect.

This last point is very important. It used to be employees who were efficient and effective were rewarded with promotions and pay raises. We now live in a global economy, where technology has shrunk both time and space. Technology has dramatically improved the flow of information, making workers, companies, and countries far more efficient. As a result, there is hypercompetition in all industries, and that competition is global. Workers who are efficient and effective at what they are tasked to do will get to keep their jobs, while those that are not pulling their own weight will find themselves involved in layoffs. When companies have to tighten their belts, they stack rank employees. Those that are graded at or near the bottom of the list will find themselves unemployed. It is unfortunate, but it is also inherently fair that those that are contributing the most keep their jobs, and those that are not contributing as much are forced to find something else to do.

Most people give up once the sailing gets a little choppy. Developing the habit of persistence goes a long way toward the achievement of anything worthwhile. You'll recall the story of my high school basketball career in Chapter 2. That whole situation was beyond ridiculous. I'd be lying to you if I didn't admit the thought of quitting didn't creep into my mind once or twice. I remember talking to my high school baseball coach (Wayne Johnson) midway through the basketball season of my senior year. Behind Coach Huse, Coach Johnson was the second most knowledgeable guy I ever played for in organized sports. He also knew a little something about character, persistence, and leadership—things far more important than baseball. We were talking one day after school as I was on my way to basketball practice, and he could sense I was extremely dejected with how the basketball season was going. I think he also sensed the thought of quitting had crossed my mind. He told me under the circumstances, he wouldn't think any less of me if I quit.

"But I'd leave you with this," he said. "The easiest thing in the world to do is to quit. Anybody can do that. Not just anybody has the character to see things through to the end, especially when things are not going the way you want them to." Needless to say, I eliminated the word "quit" from my vocabulary and mind right then and there. What a great, succinct message to send to a kid.

Another aspect of work ethic is being aggressive. You've no doubt heard the saying, nice guys finish last. While that isn't necessarily true, there is genius in being bold and taking action. As you get older, you will have far more regrets for the things you didn't do than the things you did do.

I had the opportunity to hear Lou Holtz speak in the late 1990s in Indianapolis. Coach Holtz was a highly successful college football coach, where he amassed an overall record of 249-132-7. He spent 11 seasons at Notre Dame, where he is #2 all-time in wins, second only to the great Knute Rockne. He was coaching at Notre Dame at the time, and he told a story of swimming in a lake with some friends when he was in grade school. As he told in the story, the lake was about a mile wide. Several of his friends made a bet with each other that they could swim across the lake. One of his friends began to struggle about three-quarters of the way across the lake. Fearing he could not make it the whole way, the boy turned back. Since he had made it that far, he knew he could make it back to shore where he started. *As it turned out, the boy ended up swimming a mile and a half because he didn't believe he could swim a mile.* Think about that for a moment. He ended up swimming 50 percent farther than he set out to do because he turned back. How many times do we adults do similar things out of fear or due to a lack of self-confidence? A few examples are below:

- How many adults don't go back to school to improve their economic lives because they are too busy watching television? In other words, they turned back.

- How many adults are afraid to ask for a better price when purchasing a big-ticket item because they are afraid of conflict? In other words, they turned back.

- How often do adults live unhappy lives because they are afraid to confront their problems, be it relationship issues, substance abuse issues, or obesity? In other words, they turned back.

- How many adults don't throw their name in the hat for a job with more responsibility and more money because they are afraid of rejection or afraid they might fail? In other words, they turned back.

"One can choose to go back toward safety or forward toward growth. Growth must be chosen again and again; fear must be overcome again and again."

Abraham Maslow, Psychologist

Another example of the power of simply being aggressive can be traced back to World War II. Everyone has heard of the tragic bombing of Pearl Harbor on December 7, 1941. Or if you are a history buff, you could recite the date of D-Day or the date the Japanese surrendered. However, one of the most critical dates in the entire war was April 18, 1942. It was on this day the United States launched a surprise attack on Tokyo in retaliation for the Pearl Harbor raid. The US launched sixteen B-25 medium bombers from the aircraft carrier Hornet around 8:00 a.m. local time. The raid was designed to hit as many military targets as they could. However, in the grand scheme of things, the raid produced little strategic value. What the raid did accomplish is change the outlook on the entire war for both countries.

Up until the Tokyo bombing, the US was tentative and had suffered several defeats in battle in the Pacific theatre. This caused the US to be unsure of herself, and therefore lacked the belief she could win. After the Tokyo bombing, it was the Japanese who, for the first time, began to allow seeds of doubt to creep in, and they pulled back a bit. Also, for the first time, the US believed she could win and surged forward. Compared to Pearl Harbor, the Tokyo bombing was a mere pinprick, yet many historians believe it changed the entire complexion of the war. The US surged forward, while the Japanese turned back.

The difference between success and failure can often be broken down into these simplistic terms: do you find yourself in the habit of surging forward or turning back?

A Collection of Thoughts

Think about a few successes you've had in your own life. This could be anything—a good grade in school, leading your team in scoring in a basketball game, or getting a date with the cutest girl in your class. Did you surge forward when faced with adversity? Did you overcome your fear of failure or rejection by taking positive action? Did you grit your teeth and work harder when the going got tough?

Conversely, think of a few failures or setbacks you've experienced. Did you, in fact, turn back when the going got tough? Did you let up because you thought defeat was inevitable? Does adversity cause you to turn back, or do you redouble your efforts and surge forward? It's been said your attitude determines your altitude. History is full of stories where this is, in fact, the case. Developing the habit of surging forward, of not giving up, will force lady luck to your side—sometimes when you least expect it. As I stated earlier, the harder I work, the luckier I get. I happen to believe in luck.

(3)Commitment to Continuous Learning

At some point, you will begin a professional career. You will find many jobs contain a tremendous amount of responsibilities. As companies continue to try and do more with less, you will find efficiency and effectiveness will be the ultimate measuring stick upon which decisions are made on who gets promoted and who makes the most money. Or, in a down economy, who gets to keep their job and who is let go. Now, what is the difference between efficiency and effectiveness? In short, efficiency is doing things right, and effectiveness is doing the right things.

Thus, critical success factors are at the heart of efficiency and effectiveness. It's encouraging to know we can break down just about any job into 5 to 7 key tasks or key result areas you must be competent in if you're going to be successful in that role. Rarely will there be more than that. If you find yourself attempting to be highly effective at more than 5 to 7 things, relook at what you're trying to accomplish. You may be trying to do too much. In some cases, LESS is MORE.

For example, if you are a salesperson, your key result areas will look something like this:

- Prospecting
- Qualifying
- Questioning skills
- Proposal generation

A Collection of Thoughts

- Presentation skills
- Objection handling
- Negotiating skills

The point here is self-improvement can't happen until you know what skills and key result areas you need to be focused on in the first place. You can't hit a target you can't see. By understanding specifically what areas you need to excel at, you are essentially providing yourself a track to run on, and thus significantly improving your chance for success.

Another point worth mentioning is that as you start your career, *what you learn is more important than what you make*. Now, make no mistake; income is very important. You certainly want to get paid fairly for your contributions and level of responsibility. That said, early in your career, don't let money be the sole deciding factor in where you work or what job you take. It may make sense to take a job where you think you can learn the most, that has the most accomplished leadership team, or that has a more robust training program, even if it's for a little less money.

If you ever find yourself in a job where you aren't exactly sure what is expected, then go ask your immediate manager. If you think you know what is important in your job, you should still run your list by your manager to make sure the two of you are on the same page. You don't want to work hard at a key result area or two only to find out your company or manager didn't think those areas were important. The biggest waste of time is to do a task well that need not have been done at all.

Along the lines of self-improvement, a true professional conducts self-evaluations in each one of these areas on an ongoing basis. In many cases, if you're not getting the overall results you are looking for, you might find you need to improve in just one area to significantly improve your overall performance. That is to say, sometimes it's just one key result area that is holding you back. Eliminating one bottleneck can leapfrog you forward to your desired results.

A self-evaluation might be as simple as rating yourself from 1 to 10 in each area. You might want to have your manager, a customer, or co-worker rate you as well to ensure you are getting a 360-degree feedback loop. You can then rate the key result areas in terms of importance, and in terms of how you rated yourself. Armed with some quantifiable data at your fingertips, you now know where to focus your self-improvement efforts. This evaluation might look like the following table. We'll stick with our salesperson example from above.

Skill	Importance	Skill Rating (1-10)	Steps to Get Better
Prospecting	1	9	
Qualifying 2	2	**4**	
Questioning Skills	3	7	
Proposal Generation	4	8	
Presentation Skills	5	9	
Objection Handling	6	6	
Negotiating Skills	7	5	

As you can see, in our example, we rated ourselves as only a 4 out of 10 in the area of Qualifying. In sales, it's well known you can't waste time chasing parked cars. You need to be able to determine, and quickly, whether a prospect is a good fit for what your company does, and determine if they have the money to pay for it. This is a vital skill in a selling situation. So, a simple chart like the one above can help you identify and focus on which skill you need to improve upon.

Additionally, continuous improvement requires a disciplined approach to getting better. Going back to the example above, once you've raised your Qualifying Skills to a 7 or 8, then go to work on the next lowest rated skill (in this example, Negotiating Skills). Going through this exercise continually will catapult you to the top of your field. One thing I've tried to do throughout my career is to schedule thirty minutes per day to read. I use this time to learn, to find one or two ideas I can use to get better at what I do. I've never relied on what many call luck. *I have found fortune is temporary, but knowledge is permanent.* Dedicating time to learn on a continual basis will produce knowledge, and knowledge is worth its weight in gold.

One final thought: your Grandpa Johns gave a little book to me in June 1994, and he said, "Mike, I have had this for years and read it periodically. It covers the basics very well." The following passage was written some time ago by H. K. Dugdale. It will serve you well throughout your career.

How To Make The Most Out Of Your Job

It may surprise you to know that *you are richer than you think!* And if you'll give me about fifteen minutes of your time, I'll try to prove it to you.

This little book has just one purpose: to help you become more successful, in whatever your work happens to be – regardless of who you are, what your particular job is, or what company you work for. So, read it carefully.

First of all, I'm sure you'll agree that it takes time to do anything well.

It takes time to succeed, because "success" is merely the perfectly natural reward for taking the time to do things well.

Now time is the most valuable thing in the world! But – did you ever stop to realize that you have just as much of this valuable commodity, time, as the richest man who ever lived! Neither Thomas Edison, Henry Ford, Andrew Carnegie nor John D. Rockefeller had any more time than you have. It was the way in which they used their time that made them successful.

Today – each one of us, you and I, and every man and woman who works in your company, has exactly the same amount of time – the same twenty-four hours a day.

So it stands to reason that whether we succeed or fail, or just stand still in our jobs, depends on what we do with those twenty-four hours – how we use them to get the most out of our jobs – by putting the most into them – and how we use our leisure time as well.

Those twenty-four hours are like nuggets of gold! We can fitter them away, and they do no one any good, or we can invest them wisely in ways that will not only enrich us, but help others too.

If you want to discover how to succeed on your twenty-fours a day – read every word – and – as you read check with a pencil the ideas you feel will be most helpful to you in making the most out of your job.

Take time to read it NOW!

1. Take Time To Think
It is the shortest and surest way to success in any job; it cuts down costly mistakes; it makes one's work more interesting – less tiring. Before you act take time to THINK.

2. Take Time To Be Thorough
"Good enough" is not enough in today's keen competition for success. The men and women and companies who are getting ahead today are those who take time to be thorough and painstaking in everything they do.

3. Take Time To Cooperate
Cooperation is the magic key to getting along with people – the secret to getting things done. There can be no successful work without TEAMWORK.

4. Take Time To Give And Take Orders – Cheerfully
Everyone who works, from office boy to president, is responsible for either taking, or giving orders. Often it isn't easy, or pleasant. But, it helps us and everyone concerned, if we take time to do it cheerfully.

5. Take Time To Finish What You Start
The world is full of "starters" but it's the "finishers" who win out in the end. Jumping from one unfinished job to another gets us nowhere and confuses everyone around us. FINISH IT! Take time to do one thing at a time.

6. Take Time To Get The Facts
Guesswork has wrecked many a business, ruined many an otherwise successful career. Always take time to get the facts about every problem; hear both sides of every argument with an open mind; avoid snap judgment; ask for advice when you are not sure.

7. Take Time To Plan
By planning your work in an orderly way, it makes things easier for YOU and for every fellow worker who looks to you for leadership.

8. Take Time To Know Your Company
No matter what your job may be, you are important to your company. Make sure that you know your company – its business, its aims, its problems and operation. Your day's work will take on new meaning for your when you realize that you are a part of your company.

A Collection of Thoughts

9. Take Time To Explain
In talking with others about their work be specific, be clear, explain just what you mean and, if practical, give reasons. We all do our best work when we understand just what we are expected to do – and why. Even a child asks "Why?"

10. Take Time To Listen
You'll find it the best way to acquire knowledge, and experience – and incidentally, to become popular. By being a good listener, you let others know that you are interested in them, their problems, their ideas and the progress.

11. Take Time To Answer Questions
When people ask you questions about their work, their company, encourage them. It's a healthy sign. Such people want to get ahead – by learning. Take time to answer their questions and guide them in any way you can.

12. Take Time To Put First Things First
You will get ahead faster, and find more satisfaction in your work, if you do everything in the order of its importance. You'll be surprised how much time you save, and how many little things are of no real importance at all.

13. Take Time To Praise
Go out of you way, if necessary, to compliment anyone who has done an outstanding job. That's the spirit that helps men and women succeed, by making them try even harder next time.

14. Take Time To Do It Now
Don't put it off – don't procrastinate. The longer you do the more difficult it will seem. Let people know they can depend on you to get things done – NOW. Your example will inspire them to do likewise.

15. Take Time To Admit And Correct Your Mistakes
We all make mistakes, at times. In fact we learn by our mistakes – provided we understand, and correct them; and see that we avoid the greater mistake of trying to excuse them with 'alibis.'

16. Take Time To Be On Time
Promptness is a virtue which every business has a right to expect in the people it employs. When we are habitually behind time we

usually are careless and indifferent in other ways as well. Make promptness a habit – it saves time in the end.

17. Take Time To Make People Feel Important
"What's the use" is the attitude of the person who has not been shown the importance of what he is doing. Just as every job is important, so is every person who has a job. In talking, and working with people, avoid above all things making them feel small, inconsequential.

18. Take Time To Be Neat
Untidiness and carelessness go hand in hand. An untidy desk, office, workbench, ship, or store reflects indifferent thinking on the part of the person responsible. Personal neatness (not dressiness) is important too. Neatness takes a little time but is pays big dividends.

19. Take Time To Be Courteous
To fellow workers, to customers, to everyone with whom you have contact. It makes people glad to know you – glad to work with you – and glad to help you to get ahead.

20. Take Time To Be Concise
Make it clear but make it snappy. Don't waste time by wasting words. Know what you want to say, and say it, clearly, so the other fellow knows just what you mean. You'll save his time, and your own.

21. Take Time To Understand The "Other Fellow"
Talk things over with him – get his viewpoints; try to understand his problems and the reasons for his grievances. Better understanding is the key to all successful human relations – in and out of business.

22. Take Time To Do Your Best
"Average" people are always in a plentiful supply – but what every business needs, to grow successfully, is more better-than-average people, who take time to do their best. No one has ever been able to do more – nor has anyone ever won real success by doing less.

23. Take Time To Be Patient
An impatient attitude toward our own work, or the work of others, not only slows us down, but everyone around us as well. Success demands patience.

24. Take Time To Remember
"I forgot" has robbed many a man of success. Forgetfulness causes

mistakes (sometimes catastrophes) and mistakes cost money, in any business. People who remember what they are told can be depended upon to get ahead.

25. Take Time To Be Efficient
By reducing wasted motions efficiency helps us to work more easily, with less fatigue; enables us to do more work in the same time, or the same work in less time. That's why promotion is usually based on efficiency.

26. Take Time To Look For The Best In People
You'll be doubly rewarded. This attitude toward those we work with makes work more pleasant for them – and for us – and helps us both progress. People gladly do more for us, and for the company, in an atmosphere of trust and human understanding.

27. Take Time To Avoid Gossip
Don't listen to it; don't participate in it – just walk away from it. And that goes for "office politics" too.

28. Take Time To Keep Your Temper
Don't lose it. The day's work often presents difficulties, petty annoyances, misunderstandings. Don't let them get you down. No one ever accomplished anything by "flying off the handle." Someone wisely said that "A man is no bigger than the things that get his goat."

29. Take Time To Make Intelligent Decisions
When decisions have to be made, whether of major or minor importance, make sure that they are well thought out – from all angles. Many a good job, or an entire business, has been lost due to faulty, spur-of-the-moment decisions.

30. Take Time To Be Tolerant
It takes all kinds of people, and all sorts of ideas, to make a world – or even a business organization. We don't have to agree with the other fellow's opinions, but it pays to be tolerant of them. Harmony and tolerance within an organization are essential to its success, and to yours.

31. Take Time To Be Careful
In the high speed world of today it isn't always easy, but carefulness pays big dividends in better work and a better feeling about our work. Success is not often won by carelessness.

A Collection of Thoughts

32. Take Time To Live Up To Your Promises
Let everyone with who you work know that you can always be relied upon to do what you say.

33. Take Time To Say "Thank You"
No matter who you are, or what your position, try making it a habit to say "thank you" whenever anyone does anything for you. There's no one so big, or so small, as not to appreciate it – and somehow, it does something for us, too.

34. Take Time To Be Enthusiastic
Enthusiasm is contagious. One person's enthusiasm can inspire an entire organization to more successful effort. Do everything you do with enthusiasm. It kills boredom – it banishes "that tired feeling" and generates success.

35. Take Time To Express Your Honest Opinion
Don't be a "yes" man. If you have an opinion of your own, express it. Every business needs new ideas, and constructive opinions. They are the foundation of progress.

36. Take Time To Keep Your Eyes On Your Goal
Don't be a wobbler! Set a goal for yourself and concentrate your attention and your effort on reaching that goal – one step at a time.

37. Take Time To Be Human
While it is true that "business is business" – business is also people – and people are human. The human touch in business makes for better human relations, all down the line. Try it and see.

38. Take Time To Make Helpful Suggestions
Every business needs constructive suggestions, for improving its operation, or its products, and every normal person appreciates helpful suggestions about his work. Suggest, don't criticize.

39. Take Time To Smile
Smile when you give instructions – smile when you talk to customers – it's a wonderful way to win cooperation and friends.

40. Take Time For Self Improvement
When we stop going ahead we start drifting backward. A few minutes each day, devoted to improving ourselves, pays tremendous dividends in personal progress and happiness.

A Collection of Thoughts

41. Take Time To Take Care Of Your Health
No matter how much money or material wealth you may have, good health is the most valuable asset of all. Guard your health. You can't buy it back if you lose it, or win success without it.

42. Take time To Acquire a Hobby
It will not only increase our enjoyment of the spare time you have today, but it will give you something to look forward to when you retire.

43. Take Time To Save
It is the shortest and safest road to independence, security, and self-respect. Put aside a fixed percentage of every dollar every payday. Don't go into debt for things you don't need. Take time to ask yourself "can I afford it?"

44. Take Time To Relax
Not even a machine can keep going at high speed forever. Relax after work; relax at lunch time; relax when you go to bed at night and try to get eight hours of sound, relaxed sleep. A little relaxation generates a lot of valuable energy. It is nature's way of "recharging our batteries."

45. Take Time To Learn
There are countless things to learn about your work, your company, about people – what's going on in the world, etc. Even things which seem to have no direct bearing on your job today may be of tremendous value tomorrow. Don't let your mind get in a rut – take time to keep on learning.

46. Take Time To Make Friends
"Friends are life's jewels." Friends are invaluable both in our business, and social life. Never let old friendships die and never stop making new friends.

47. Take Time To Enjoy Your Family
When you go home, leave your business behind you. Concentrate on your family and its interests. They'll thank you for it and you'll be better on the job tomorrow.

48. Take Time To Be Kind
Be kind in little ways. Be kind to strangers, to newcomers in the organization, to people in trouble – and especially to people who least expect it. A little kindness can generate a lot of cooperation.

49. Take Time To Read
Don't let the television monopolize all your spare time. Do some worthwhile reading on your own and take time to mentally digest what you read. An active mind is mighty good job insurance.

50. Take Time To Be Thankful
Be thankful that you live in America – that you have a job; that you are free to think as you please; to work where you please; to worship God wherever and whenever you please. Thankfulness for what you have paves the way for more and bigger blessings.

51. Take Time To Understand Your Job
Whatever it is – wherever it is – it is your job and what you make of it depends on one person – YOU. Be sure that you know the reason for your job – what makes it important to other people, to your company, and to you. The best way to earn promotion to a better job tomorrow, is to understand, and master, the job you have today.

52. Take Time To Have Faith
– faith that you can, and will, succeed in your work – that you can help others to succeed in their work, and that your life will be a successful, satisfying experience, if you "Take Time" to do these things.

A Helpful Suggestion
Now that you have learned the secret of "How To Make The Most Out Of Your Job" I want to offer a practical suggestion – to help you get the full benefit from it. Put this booklet aside for thirty days.

Then read it, and re-check it once a month, until you have acquired the habit of taking time to do those things which you may have been neglecting.

Yes – it will take some time, but you couldn't invest it to better advantage."

H. K. Dugdale
(*How to Make the Most Out of Your Job*)

(4) Exceptional Time Management

Peter Drucker once said, "Until you can manage time, you can manage nothing else." Ask yourself this question frequently, "Am I spending time or investing time?" The differences over time are dramatic. As Michael Altshuler once said, "The bad news is time flies. The good news is you're the pilot."

You've no doubt heard of compound interest. The Collins English dictionary defines compound interest as "interest calculated on both the principal and the accrued interest." Albert Einstein is sometimes said to have called compound interest "the greatest mathematical discovery of all time." Similar to how the compound interest of money begins to grow exponentially over time, focusing your efforts on a few key result areas, on truly important activities, has a compounding effect on the results you achieve.

As an example, let's say you are investing one hour per day reading books and whitepapers in an effort to become an expert in your chosen field. This has a multiplying, compound effect over time.

- You read a book and pick up two or three new ideas that you can immediately implement in your own work.

- You read one book, and the author recommends several other books that you end up reading. You've now doubled or tripled the number of ideas you can implement.

- By reading, you are expanding your vocabulary.

- This commitment to continuous learning has improved your job performance, and therefore your income. This motivates you to learn even more, so you keep right on learning. Committing a little bit of time, daily, starts to have a snowball effect on your entire life.

Focusing on your goals will help you stay focused on *investing time* versus *spending time*. We all need free time or downtime once in a while. We all need hobbies and things that enable us to relax and recharge our batteries. But watch closely how you are using your time. Watching a football game on TV is a great way to relax. But if you find yourself watching college football from 12:00 p.m. until 12:00 a.m. on a Saturday, this would be an example of spending time, not investing time. Golf is another great way to get some fresh air and spend some quality time with a friend. Golfing once per week is a terrific way to unwind. But, if you find yourself playing several rounds of golf per week, or sneaking out of work early multiple times per week to play golf, this would be an example of spending time.

Conversely, if you are setting aside one hour per day to read subjects in your field (finance, leadership, sales, technical whitepapers), this would be an example of investing your time. It has been said *the average adult after graduating from high school doesn't read a single book the remainder of their life.* If you simply read 30 minutes per day, five days per week, on average, you would conservatively read one book per month. That equates to 12 books per year. Over a five year period, this translates into more than 60 books. If you generated just three ideas per book, that equates to more than 180 new ideas you can apply to your life, work, and career. I promise you, the average adult doesn't come up with 180 ideas in a lifetime, much less in five years. If you did that and took the best ideas you learned and applied those to your work, do you think that would make a difference in your career? You bet it would! Do you think that would have an impact on your income? Absolutely! *Over time, this habit is like compound interest; it compounds and multiplies.*

If you want to know exactly how you are using your time, try keeping track of it for a week or a month. Track how many hours per day you spend watching TV. Track everything:

- Work
- Exercise
- Church
- Reading
- Pleasure activities
- Watching TV
- Travel time/Daily commute to work
- Running errands

Once you understand exactly how you are spending or investing your time, you will know where you can make improvements. Regarding time management, this exercise alone would likely be more valuable than any training course you could attend. Also, you might do this periodically, say one time per year. Tracking your time periodically in this manner is a good way to ensure you stay focused on the most important things and don't get too far off track with unproductive activities.

For example, let's say you are closely tracking your time and realize you spend, on average, one hour per day commuting between home and work. But as you analyze this, you also realize you are driving during rush hour. By leaving 15 minutes early, or staying at work 15 minutes later, your commute is cut down from 60 minutes to 45 minutes (a 25 percent reduction). And, let's say you decide to spend those 45 minutes in the car listening to audio programs on motivation, time management, leadership, selling skills, or some other self-improvement program. *What have you accomplished?*

- Reduced your commute time by 15 minutes, or 1 hour and 15 minutes per week. Do you think this would be beneficial?

- You're working 30 minutes longer per day, or two and a half hours per week. Assuming you took off three weeks for vacation, this adds 122.5 hours per year (2.5 hrs. x 49 weeks). This equates to an additional three work weeks per year. Would this help you be more successful?

- By turning drive time into learning time, you're investing 45 minutes per day in self-improvement and education, or 3 hours and 45 minutes per week. Would this help?

This is the kind of time leverage that can make a huge difference over time. And we accomplished this simply by analyzing how we are using our time, and in this case, just one aspect of our day (our daily commute).

Years ago, I was attending a half-day seminar on time management. To kick off the day, the speaker pulled out a large glass pitcher and filled it with rocks. He asked the audience if we thought the pitcher was full. We all agreed the pitcher was full. He then poured sand in it, and to my amazement, it didn't overfill. He then asked the audience again, is it full? We all agreed it had to be full now. He then pulled out a pitcher of water, and he poured that into the glass pitcher we assumed twice now was already full. Once again, it didn't overfill. The point to the story is there is never enough time to get everything done, but there is always enough time to get the most important things done.

A few ideas, while quite simple, can be helpful to ensure you maintain complete control over your time. You can:

- Use to-do lists
- Prioritize your tasks as to their urgency and importance
- Eliminate low-value tasks

Use To-do Lists

The greatest waste of time is to do something well that need not have been done at all. Take time to plan your work before you jump in. Give careful thought to what you need to do. If you're working on a large project, break it down into smaller steps, and determine in what order each step needs to be completed. This additional step in planning will save an enormous amount of time. *It's been said an ounce of prevention is worth a pound of cure.* This is especially true with your time.

By working off of to-do lists, you will ensure you are not distracted by phone calls, email, or a co-worker who wants to chit-chat. A well-organized to-do list will keep you on track and keep you focused on your most important tasks. It also helps you work in straight lines and keeps you from needlessly getting distracted. For example, let's say you have five to six things you want to accomplish over a weekend around the house. Maybe your list looks something like this:

1. Reorganize a trash drawer in the kitchen.
2. Clean out a closet.
3. Clean out the garage.
4. Go through an attic to give away old clothes.
5. Fertilize the lawn.
6. Change the bed sheets.

The mere act of writing things down dramatically increases the likelihood you will do it. There is an emotional bond, a sense of accomplishment, to be able to check things off your list as you complete them. The same phenomenon works with goals. Once you have committed something to paper, and review it regularly, these unfinished items tug on you to complete them whether you feel like it or not.

Prioritize Your Time

There is never enough time to get everything done that needs your attention. However, there is always enough time to get the most important things done. You have the same 24 hours per day the most successful people in the world have. The difference is how you spend those 24 hours. Are you *spending* it or *investing* it? Once you have a completed your to-do list, review which tasks are the most important. Decide which task is the most important, and do that first. Then take the second most important task, and do that one next, and so on.

A helpful way to prioritize your tasks is to think in terms of *urgent* versus *important*. The following table will serve as an illustration for our discussion.

Time Management Magic Quadrant

Urgent but not Important (yellow)	**Urgent and Important** (green)
Neither Urgent nor Important (red)	**Important but not Urgent** (green)

Urgent and Important (Green Quadrant)

A good time management technique is to always first spend time in the upper right quadrant of the box above. The more time you can spend in this quadrant, the better. If you're not sure how important something is, ask yourself, "What are the consequences if this task does not get completed?" If the consequences are minimal, then maybe you should not be doing it. Another question to ask, especially if you are in a leadership position, is, "Can someone else do this task instead of me?" If someone else can accomplish the task at least 80 percent as effectively as you can, then delegate it. Remember, we need to be investing our time, not spending it. Be very careful about how you are using your time.

Another thing to keep in mind is this: *if something has to be done eventually, then you might as well do it immediately.* Don't put off tasks that might not be fun or tasks that make you a little uncomfortable. Do the things that must be done first. Start your day doing the most important things on your to-do list. If you do, then the rest of your day becomes much easier.

Important but not Urgent (Green Quadrant)

Sometimes there are urgent tasks that you have to tend to right away. While urgent tasks frequently do need our attention, I'd make a couple of suggestions:

- Ask yourself, "Do I really need to be doing this urgent task, or can I delegate the task to someone else?"

- What would happen if you did nothing? Early in my career, my manager left me a voicemail needing something right away. I happened to be traveling at the time and could not respond right away. As it turned out, my manager was able to get the information he was looking for on his own. Now, I'm not advocating ignoring your manager, but it did teach me a valuable lesson. Before you drop everything you're doing to complete a task for someone else, make sure it's important, and make sure you understand the timeline for completing the task. You'd be surprised how often throughout my career what appears to be important or urgent, turns out to be neither. There's an old saying along these lines, "Failure to plan on your part does not necessarily create an emergency on my part."

This is perhaps the most important quadrant. These tasks are important, but because they are not urgent, it is easy to put them off. A few examples:

- Reading 30 minutes per day in your chosen field
- Reviewing long-term goals
- Revising plans to achieve your goals
- Exercising 30 minutes per day to improve your health

The reason it's easy to put these types of tasks off is because there isn't an immediate consequence for not doing them. To ensure this doesn't happen, make sure you are scheduling Important but not Urgent tasks on your calendar. Treat these calendar entries as a meeting, and stick to it. If you were meeting with a client, you would never just blow that off. The same is true here. Once an important task is on your calendar, you are far more likely to do it.

Urgent but not Important (Yellow Quadrant)

Urgent tasks are things that need to be done right away, but they may not be important. Examples of this include the following:

- You see you have an email, voicemail, or text message, and you feel the need to check it right away.
- A co-worker asks you for a favor while you are in the middle of doing something important. You want to be a supportive teammate and coworker, but ask yourself, "Can this wait?"
- You have a stack of mail that you need to open and review.

There are some tasks that are not important to you personally, but you need to do them. As a suggestion, block out time on your calendar for routine tasks and do those tasks only during the scheduled time. This block of time might include things like checking email, checking voicemail, reviewing your mail, and returning messages. By grouping like tasks together, you accomplish the following:

- You complete these tasks more quickly when like tasks are grouped together.
- You improve your overall productivity by not constantly starting and stopping your work on important tasks.

Neither Urgent nor Important (Red Quadrant)

Obviously, we want to avoid doing anything in this quadrant. If something is neither urgent nor important, then it's a complete waste of time, and therefore should not be done at all. Examples in a workplace setting might be the following:

- Reading the newspaper
- Talking to friends on the phone
- Participating in gossip in the coffee room
- Playing games on the internet

Here is an exercise. Make a list of all of the things you do on a typical day. Think through your routine at work and what you do while you're at home. Then, start to transpose this list on to the Magic Quadrant table. You can quickly get a visual as to how much of your time is being spent on important things. *It's also an effective way to see if you are investing time or spending time.* People who invest their time spend a disproportionate amount of their time in the green quadrants. People who are merely spending their time spend an inordinate amount of their time in the yellow or red quadrants. *Don't confuse activity with productivity.* Whatever you're doing, make sure it is important, and it gets you closer to your goals.

Posteriorities

This may be a new term for you. Think of a posteriority as the opposite of a priority. A posteriority is something that you should stop doing to free up more time for important tasks (sounds familiar?). In other words, posteriorities are low-value tasks. They are activities that do not bring us closer to our goals.

Following the theme of our Magic Quadrant of time management, posteriorities would be tasks and activities that we would find in the red quadrant. A few examples are below:

- Coming home from work and watching TV for several hours
- Going out to clubs after work for several hours and drinking excessively
- Playing video games for hours on end
- Spending (there's that word again) an inordinate amount of time social networking on sites like Facebook or Twitter
- Spending hours mindlessly surfing the internet

If you want to spend more time on important tasks that bring you closer to your goals, a good first step is to analyze how you are currently spending your time. As you analyze your time, ask yourself what kinds of activities can you eliminate to free up more time to spend on more important, high-value tasks. *Eliminating low-value tasks is just as important as identifying what high-value tasks and activities you should be doing.*

(5) Take Time to Think

While I was very fortunate to marry the woman of my dreams, I didn't get married until I was 33. I began working for Xerox when I was 23. Thus, I had a ten-year period where I could focus exclusively on myself and my career. Without the demands of a young family, I was able to put this time to good use.

- I worked very hard, routinely working more than 60 hours per week. Thus, compared to someone my age working 40 hours per week, I was netting an additional 50 percent more experience in the same amount of time. This was huge. I've often said I gained 10 years of experience in my first 3 years at Xerox.
- Obtained my MBA in an after-hours Executive program.
- Read constantly on subjects like sales, management, and leadership. In fact, I built a small library at home based on all the books I read.
- Experimented with new ideas with a few teams I was leading (self-directed work teams, empowerment, recognition).
- Transitioned from operations management to sales and on to sales management.

- Succeeded some.

- Failed some, but wasn't afraid to try new things.

- Learned a lot, and I mean A LOT!

- Saw my income grow nearly 10 times in 10 years!

During these ten years, what I learned, and how I developed both personally and professionally, had a lot to do with the making of this book. Now, I'm not suggesting you shouldn't get married at a younger age. I'm simply pointing out this ten-year period proved very beneficial to me.

As you begin to develop goals and move on in your career, you will find it invaluable to *take time to think and plan*. Taking some additional time upfront to think and plan almost always saves time in the end. It can also eliminate costly mistakes. Bouncing around from one idea to another that wasn't well thought out in advance, starting and stopping, takes up a lot more time than getting it right the first time. My dad used to say "measure twice and cut once." Thinking and planning enables you to "cut once." It also eliminates starting and stopping, and enables you to work in straight lines versus bouncing around all over the place. The shortest distance between two points is a straight line, so always try and work in straight lines. You've heard the story of the turtle and the hare, where they compete in a running race. The turtle, while slow, gives it his all, never stops running, and he stays on course, he runs in straight lines. Meanwhile, the hare runs in zig-zags, stops to pick flowers, starts running again, stops to talk to a friend, starts running again…you get the point. Ultimately the turtle beats the much faster hare in the race because he runs in straight lines and never stops.

Thinking and planning enables you to do the same thing. I've seen many people run a hundred miles an hour, from one task to another, constantly starting and stopping, but never really getting anything done. Far better to plan in advance, work quickly, and work in straight lines. You will make far fewer mistakes, avoid starting and stopping, and ultimately accomplish far more in a shorter amount of time. The legendary college basketball coach John Wooden used to say, "Be quick, but don't hurry." There is a subtle genius in this statement.

We mentioned earlier the only real limits to what you can have, be, or do, are the limits you place on yourself. If you aren't getting the results you are looking for, you may need to:

A Collection of Thoughts

- Work a little harder
- Apply more discipline
- Acquire more knowledge
- Improve your skills
- Acquire new abilities
- Generate new ideas
- Manage your time better

Keep in mind, the only variables to obtaining the things mentioned above are effort and time. You have full control over both.

You've no doubt heard the idea of *brainstorming*. This is a highly effective way to think. Brainstorming involves getting a legal pad of paper, getting in a quiet room with no distractions, and writing down your goal or a problem you are trying to solve at the top of the sheet. Then begin thinking of everything you can do to obtain your goal or solve your problem. Whatever comes to mind, write it down, no matter how crazy the idea may seem. During a brainstorming session, we are not evaluating any of the ideas we come up with, but simply writing down anything and everything that comes to mind. If you have an idea, don't think, "Well, that will never work." Write it down anyway. After you're done brainstorming, you can begin to pick and choose which ideas to use and which ones to discard.

You will find it is very easy to generate ideas initially, but after five or ten minutes, it starts to become harder. It is precisely when it gets hard to think of something new that you really have to dig deep and can sometimes have a break-through idea. If you are trying to solve a complex problem, you may spend several days before you come up with a good solution.

Thinking is one of the most exhaustive things humans can do. Thinking and concentrating can be more exhausting than hard, physical labor. This is probably why only 3 percent of the population are strategic thinkers. Given this can be draining, I would limit your brainstorming sessions to 30 minutes at a time (likely once per day). Anything beyond 30 minutes will likely begin to have diminishing returns. Brainstorming with a legal pad and pen is a tremendous tool toward success and goal achievement.

Life Lessons

- Take your career seriously, but not yourself.

- In addition to having clearly defined, written goals, you should always have a plan of attack on how you are going to improve in your key result areas. This one discipline will catapult you into the Top 3 percent of your field.

- Make sure you are investing time, not spending time.

- Always maintain a sense of urgency. Those that do get far more done than those that don't. In your career, you'll be rewarded and promoted largely based on productivity and efficiency.

- Schedule Important and Urgent, and Important but not Urgent tasks on your calendar, and stick to this as if it was a client appointment.

- Take time to think, to plan, and to brainstorm. This will save you an enormous amount of time and put your goal-seeking efforts into hyperdrive.

CHAPTER

SUCCESS BLUEPRINT
MILLION DOLLAR HABITS

Throughout these pages I've attempted to provide tips and rules of thumb that can help you as you grow and advance in your own career. *By no means do I have all the answers, but my track record would suggest I do have a few.* In this chapter we'll summarize a few things as a quick reference guide.

To begin with, it's important to understand you are the captain of your own ship. You decide how you want to live, what you want to do, how you want to treat others, what career you take up, and who you live with. Don't let anyone attempt to force these things upon you.

Perhaps another thought I'd leave you with is always treat life as a journey. As I have set and achieved multiple goals throughout my life, one thing I have found to be consistently true is that the journey was more enjoyable than the actual achievement. Achieving something in life is simply the reward for the work you put in. It is the journey that ultimately provides the most satisfaction, the most fulfilment, and the many lessons that can be learned along the way. I'm a fan of Tony Robbins, who is an ultra-successful author and motivational speaker. He says "success is 80% psychology and 20% mechanics." I tend to agree. He goes on to say that life experiences can make us bigger or smaller, more wise or less wise, better able to adapt to changing circumstances or more susceptible to random events.

The point is *don't just be a manager of resources*, which in many cases are constraints, and constraints by definition are limited in nature. *Be a creator of circumstances*, a creator of the life you want to live.

- Don't settle for trying to make your piece of the pie just a little bigger. Create a bigger pie for yourself and everyone around you.

- Don't lower your standard of living to match your income. Raise your income up to match the standard of living that you want.

- Don't set goals based on what you think you can get. Set goals to get what you really want in life.

The list above is what leaders do. But, this isn't for lightweights. That is why only 3 out of 100 people achieve things of significance. If you are energetic enough, creative enough, work hard enough, and are passionate enough, *you can have, be, or do anything you want in life. There are only two variables: time and effort. And the good news is you have complete control over both.*

In an earlier chapter I mentioned the disease I like to call "excusitis." The symptoms of this disease sound something like the following:

- I can't get any breaks.
- I'm not the boss's favorite.
- I got screwed out of a job promotion.
- I don't have enough money.
- I haven't lived a charmed life.
- My company hosed me by laying me off.
- It's my lazy wife's fault I can't get ahead.

I could go on, but you get the point. Mark Twain once said "There are a thousand excuses for failure but never a good reason." People who constantly have reasons for their failures like to play the part of a victim. Don't be a victim. *People who have a PhD in self-pity never accomplish anything. If you don't like your circumstances, then change them.* You have it within your ability to change your circumstances. You can create the life you want. How? The discussion points below are a good start.

What does success look like? This is an individual question, and a very important one. Success is different for different people. Success could be defined in a number of ways:

- I'm a millionaire by the age of 40 (notice we've set a deadline).
- I am financially independent by the age of 50.
- I belong to the local country club by the age of 30.

- I donate a total of $1,000,000 to charity during my working life.
- I marry the woman of my dreams.

The late, great author Earl Nightingale once described success as "the progressive realization of a worthy ideal." Regardless, before you get started on working toward success, I would suggest spending some time thinking about *how you define success*. Decide what it is you want to have, be, and do, and then build a plan to accomplish those things.

Here's an exercise for you. Upon graduating from college, build your own bucket list. A bucket list comprises exactly what we've been talking about—what you want to have, be, or do during your lifetime. Specifically, I would suggest creating a Bucket List of 100 Things list. Again, this is the top 100 things you want to have, be, or do in your lifetime.

I read a book titled *Winning* by Lou Holtz, a famous college football coach mentioned earlier. He told a story of how he was fired from the University of Arkansas unexpectedly, despite having a winning record. Rather than feel sorry for himself, he put this time to good use. With some extra time on his hands, he put together a bucket list for himself. For him, he had things on his list such as (1) Become the head coach at the University of Notre Dame (which he did in 1986); (2) Win a national championship (which he did with Notre Dame in 1988); (3) Skydive (which he did). Anyway, his wife had returned home from running errands, and he very proudly told her about this list he had put together. She flatly replied, "I hope finding a job is somewhere on that list."

One thing you'll find as you grow, get older, and experience different things is your wants, needs, and desires may change over time. That's OK. You can change your goals and build new plans. This is not an "add water and stir" proposition. This is an exercise you will want to conduct once every one to three years. The reason this is an evergreen contract with yourself is because what's important to you at age 30 may not be important to you at age 50. When I was in my early twenties, I set a goal to have a small farm out in the country. I wanted to own about 20 acres and have some horses and cattle. Upon getting married, my wife wasn't into that sort of thing, I was in the throes of my career, and we started having kids; and I decided this goal was no longer important to me. So, don't be afraid to change your plans. Sailors have to regularly adjust their sails to take advantage of the direction of the wind. The same holds true with your goals and plans for success—they will need to be adjusted periodically as circum-stances change.

So, what is the blueprint for success? My Top 10 list below is a good start.

(1) Create a Bucket List

This is a list of the top 100 things you want to have, be, or do in your lifetime. *This is where long-term goal setting will take place.* You might want to update this list periodically. For long-term goals, the sky is the limit. Famous author Brian Tracy calls this exercise Blue Sky Thinking. Most people, if they've bothered to set goals in the first place, are not going after what they really want. They are going after what they think they can get. Don't put an artificial ceiling on what you can achieve, especially before you've even left the starting gate. Don't allow self-limiting beliefs to enter your mind. *The only real limits to what you can achieve are the ones you place on yourself.* If a goal is a challenge, then break it into smaller chunks. Don't say that something is impossible. Instead, ask yourself:

- How?
- Why not?
- Why not me?
- Instead of "impossible" think "I'm possible."
- Take time to think!
  - Think about what you want. Take time to think and plan on how to achieve what you want.
  - Do this thinking relentlessly. If you do, you will catapult yourself into the top 3 percent of your field, as most people will not do these things.

(2) Build and Maintain Desire

When you want something to the same extent your body needs air to breathe, then you will do whatever you need to do (honestly, morally, and ethically) to achieve that goal. We mentioned earlier strong desires produce strong results, whereas weak desires produce weak results. Develop a white-hot level of desire, and the world will be yours for the taking. Or, as my Grandpa Johns used to say, "You'll have the world by the tail in a downhill pull."

How do you create desire? One way is to track your progress and compete against yourself. By competing against yourself, you will be in a constant state of self-improvement. *Amateurs compete against other people.*

A real pro competes against himself. Don't be the smart kid in the dumb row. Constantly be working toward a goal, and toward improving yourself. Don't settle for being better than the next guy. This attitude is self-limiting. Perpetually try to be better than yourself. Keep score. This becomes a game of *You versus Life*, and this is a pretty exciting game to play. It becomes fun to stretch and keep asking yourself, "How good can I be? What else can I accomplish?"

(3) Work Hard

There is no second effort without 100 percent effort in the first place. Show up early and often, every day. In a work setting, be the first one in the office and the last one to leave. Trust me; this will get noticed.

I have found this result to be the case in my sales career. While working for EMC, I was calling on a hospital in eastern Kentucky back in 2007. They were rolling out an Electronic Medical Record application and would be buying a large amount of data storage to support this new application. I was competing against Sun, who was the incumbent. We ultimately won the deal. Afterward, I asked the client why they chose EMC. For my final proposal, I had put a tabbed binder together, complete with technical analysis, a financial summary, competitive comparisons, payment options, and references. Prior to their decision, I had also introduced them to our Project Manager so they could get comfortable with the actual people that would be doing the work should we be selected. We put a lot of effort into the sales campaign and our final proposal. My competition had simply provided quotes. The client appreciated our effort and felt we wanted their business more than my competition. Upon being awarded the project, I asked the client why they chose us. The decision-maker told me, "We figured if you were going to work harder for us on the front-end of the project, we felt you would work harder for us after the sale too." *What a great lesson—we won a $1.3 million deal simply because people recognize and appreciate hard work.* It pays to go the extra mile, literally. I found the road called the "extra mile" is really not that crowded. Most people won't go there.

(4) Maintain Persistent Discipline

If you want something badly enough, you will not allow temporary defeats or setbacks to derail you. In the confrontation between the stream and the rock, the stream always wins, not through strength, but through persistence.

If you ever find yourself in a situation where you are consistently working hard, but not getting the results you want, then get back to basics. I played baseball growing up. My dad and I used to play pepper in the backyard. Pepper is when someone pitches to you, and you take a half swing. You are simply trying to make solid contact. It trains you to keep your eye on the ball. Fast forward to my senior year in high school. I had been hitting over .400 through the first half of the season. I then hit a slump late in the year. My dad said, "When you get in a slump, get back to basics." So, despite the fact I was 18 years old, we went out in the backyard several nights and played pepper. As a result of getting back to basic fundamentals, my hitting returned late in the year.

(5) Build a Plan of Attack

To achieve anything, you have to have plans on how you will achieve your goals. Plan your work and work your plan, as the saying goes. If you wanted to build a house, your builder doesn't just show up to your lot and start building. They have a blueprint they use before they begin. They build certain parts of the house first, in sequential order. For example, you wouldn't build the roof before you build the walls. You wouldn't build the walls before you build the floors. And of course, step one in building a house is you have to build a solid foundation. The same process holds true in goal achievement. For large projects, you will likely need to break the project down into incremental steps. Prioritize this list, and then get to work, completing the project one step at a time. Always ask yourself, "What two to three things can I do today that will move me closer to my goals?"

Additionally, don't be afraid to ask for help. Whatever you are trying to accomplish, others have probably already done. Seek advice from your inner circle and others who have enjoyed success. It's been my experience successful people are almost always willing to help out if you ask them.

One final thought here. If you think you are on the right track, stick with it. Throughout my sales career, I've batted an unusually high percentage, meaning I win competitive deals disproportionally more than I lose. I had a four-year stretch from 2007–2010 where I won 85 percent of the competitive deals I was directly involved in. The average sales representative bats something closer to 30 percent. That said, I had one stretch in the fourth quarter of 2006 where I lost three of my four final deals closing out the year. I also missed my quota for the year, something I've rarely done in my sales career. My self-confidence took a pretty big dent. I took some time early in January and reviewed every sales campaign to determine what went wrong. I reviewed every proposal. I asked myself a bunch of questions. Was I at the right level? Did I understand the client's objectives? Did I match a solution to what they told me was important to them? Did I skip steps? Was the proposal well written? Did I make a pricing mistake? After a lot of analysis, I determined there was nothing wrong with my approach. I stuck with what I believed to be my fundamentals, and then promptly hit my quota for the first quarter of 2007, and went on to overachieve my quota six of the next seven years, qualifying for EMC's President's Club five times along the way.

What's the lesson? If you aren't getting the results you are looking for, don't panic; review your plan of attack. If you believe in your approach, then sometimes exhibiting a little patience is the best thing you can do.

(6) Leverage Goal Setting

Here are some ways to leverage goal setting:

- Decide exactly what you want in all areas of your life.
- Write your goals down, specifically and in the present tense, as if you have already achieved it.
- Practice the 10 Goal Exercise daily (see Chapter 4).
- Build plans, in sequential order, as to how you will achieve each goal.
- Create a sense of urgency by putting timelines on both the goal itself and the individual steps you will need to take. This will create and help maintain positive momentum. You've heard the saying a body in motion tends to stay in motion, while a body at rest tends to stay at rest. Get moving.
- Determine what resources you will need, and whose help you could use to help achieve your goals. Don't be afraid to ask for help or advice.
- Review your plans daily. Review your plans and progress on an ongoing basis. If you find yourself stuck, sometimes altering your plans just a little will enable you to leap forward.

While attending a seminar years ago, the speaker told a story about how at rest, a two-by-four board lodged against the wheels of a locomotive could keep it from moving. But if that same locomotive was traveling 60 miles per hour, it could slam through a steel-reinforced concrete wall. What's the difference? Momentum.

A Collection of Thoughts

(7) Build Unshakable Confidence

By doing the three steps below, you will be astonished at how many ideas, people, and circumstances come to your aide. You'll come up with so many ideas you'll need to keep a pen and index cards with you at all times so you can capture these ideas as they come to you. Assuming you act on these ideas, you'll be amazed at how these three steps will accelerate how quickly you achieve your goals.

- **Practice the Top 10 Goal Exercise**—Write down your top 10 goals daily in a spiral notebook. By doing this day after day, week after week, you will cement these goals into your subconscious mind. This will help you be on the alert for opportunities consistent with your goals.

- **Affirmations**—Write your goals on to 3x5 index cards and recite them to yourself every day. You might try doing this when you first wake up in the morning and right before you go to bed at night.

- **Visualization**—As you read your affirmations, add emotion to your mental images. This visualization will cement your goals deep into your subconscious mind. Your subconscious mind will then go to work on your goals for you, even while you are sleeping.

(8) Network/Ask for Help

Identify a network of successful people to interact with on a regular basis. You might schedule a coffee or lunch meeting with certain people once per month. They can be a support group to go to for advice, counsel, and to help introduce you to other influential people who might be able to help you along your journey. Two things to remember:

- **Listen**. God gave you two ears and one mouth. They should be used in that proportion. Ask other successful people for advice, and then listen to what they have to say. You learn by listening, not talking.

- **Contribute**. According to famous author Zig Ziglar, to get what you want, you must first help enough other people get what they want. Don't be selfish here; make sure you are helping others just as much as they are helping you.

(9) Read Every Day

Reading is like compound interest. As you read, you will pick up ideas on how to achieve your goals. One idea turns into another.

- **Set aside at least 30 minutes per day to read** books on your chosen field. You might also read motivational books in the event you need a shot in the arm. Keep one thing in mind: readers are leaders.

- **Drive time = learning time**. Another tip is you can listen to audio programs in your car. It is not uncommon for the average worker to spend 1 hour per day commuting to and from work. This translates into 20 hours per month or 240 hours per year of additional self-improvement. *This is the equivalent of 6 additional working weeks per year*, assuming a 40-hour workweek. This is huge time leverage. Turn drive time into learning time, and you can put your foot on the accelerator of self-development.

(10) Be Ruthless with Your Time

If you lose money, you can always make more. *You can't make more time*. Once it's gone, it's gone forever. The good news, however, is you have the same 24 hours in a day that the most successful people have. Make every hour of every day count.

- Keep a to-do list at all times, as this will help you focus on the critical few versus the trivial many. It's very easy to get distracted. A to-do list will help you focus on what's important, personally and professionally.

- Prioritize your most important tasks (see the Time Management Quadrant section in Chapter 6). Track and analyze your time periodically. Make sure you are eliminating posteriorities, so you free up time for important tasks.

- Check things off as you complete them. This action provides an emotional feeling of accomplishment.

CHAPTER

FINAL THOUGHTS
A FEW PARTING SHOTS

We've covered a lot of ground in these pages. My hope and prayer is these pages are useful to you as you grow, as you reach adulthood, and as you come across challenging situations. Life will undoubtedly force you to face tough choices from time to time. As you encounter difficult situations, there will be times when you make a bad decision. Trust me, I've made my fair share of mistakes. *Life can be an unforgiving teacher.* When mistakes are made or you fall short of something you are trying to accomplish, admit your mistake (publicly if you must), learn from the mistake or failure, dust yourself off, get back up, and move on. Failure is neither fatal nor final. The only true failure is if you quit trying.

Choose What is Right vs. What is Popular

You will also encounter occasions where what is right and what is popular are not one in the same. It takes courage to do what is right. It takes courage to follow your own convictions, your own compass, instead of following the crowd. In the middle of the Bay of Pigs crisis in October of 1962, President Kennedy is purported to have said "There is something immoral about abandoning your own judgment." You will obviously not always be right, but more often than not you will be right to follow your own belief systems and values versus someone else's.

Surround Yourself with True Friends

Another skill that will come in handy is the ability to accurately size up people, and quickly. You will occasionally run across people who enjoy watching others fail, who are quick to criticize, who are nice to people's faces but talk about them behind their back, or who do not actively try to understand someone else's point of view. People who ridicule you for your own belief systems are not true friends. These are the types of people to avoid. Make a conscious effort to surround yourself with fair-minded, honest people who are true friends, who will have your back in times of need. You will need the support of friends from time to time. It's a good idea to know who those true friends are in advance of a crisis.

Keep Don't in Your Vocabulary

And finally, keep the word "don't" in your vocabulary in the context of these seven actions:

(1) Don't be afraid to ask

(2) Don't be afraid to make decisions

(3) Don't be afraid to fail

(4) Don't be afraid to laugh at yourself

(5) Don't assume

(6) Don't be afraid to go against the grain

(7) Don't EVER be afraid to be yourself

(1) Don't be Afraid to Ask

First, ask for what you want. It's been said you miss 100 percent of the shots you don't take. It's been my experience, both personally and professionally, that *the world belongs to the askers*. I'll give you a few examples.

When I was in college, I worked one summer as a busboy for a TGI Friday's restaurant in downtown Indianapolis. At the end of the shift the busboys had to go ask the waiters/waitresses for tips, as the busboys got their tips from the waiters. I learned very quickly if you waited around for the waiters to come find you to tip you out, you would be waiting a long time. *If you wanted to get paid, you had to ask.* I was a little on the shy side at the time, but I worked very hard at that job, as I worked the downtown lunch crowd most days and it was always extremely busy. It only took getting stiffed a couple of times before I consistently summoned up the courage to ask. I put the work in, so I wasn't about to not get paid for my efforts.

Second, don't ever be afraid to *ask a question*. One of my first managers in my career was a guy named George Hodgson. He had a pet saying, "The only dumb question is the one that is not asked." If you have a question, and you're in a group setting, I'll guarantee you someone else in the room is thinking about asking the same question, but is afraid to raise their hand. You won't find out the answer if you don't ask the question. And, asking questions can save you an enormous amount of time. Don't recreate the wheel if you don't have to. If you are faced with a situation you haven't encountered before, chances are someone else has experienced whatever situation you have in front of you and can help you by sharing their own experiences with you.

A third example centers around a fraternity brother of mine named Dave Delacatto. Dave and I were members of the Alpha Kappa Lambda Fraternity at Purdue University from 1988 to 1991. Dave had a reputation for being a real lady's man. Dave was a good-looking guy, but he was by no means a Greek god. We were talking one day, and I asked him, "What's your secret with the ladies?" He told me he didn't likely bat any better percentage than the average guy, but that he simply asked (there's that word again) more women out than anybody else. As a result, he had more dates than anybody else. Ultimately, it was a numbers game. The more women he asked out, the more dates he had. It really wasn't any more complicated than that.

He also said something very interesting. The more attractive the woman, the better chance you have of getting a date with her. What??!! That makes no sense, I said. His theory was an extremely attractive woman might be a little lonely because most guys were afraid to ask a really attractive woman out, likely fearing rejection. It was this fear that led to attractive women actually having fewer dates as a result. This is counter-intuitive but makes some logical sense. An attractive woman gets asked out fewer times because most guys assume the answer will be no, or that they must already be dating someone, when in fact the opposite might be true. You don't know unless you ask. And besides, the worst outcome is that she simply says no. How harmful is that?

(2) Don't be Afraid to Make Decisions

When making decisions, particularly big decisions, there will always be some element of risk involved. Weigh your options, deliberate over the pros and cons, but *don't let fear or risk paralyze you from chasing your dreams.*

Leaders are decisive. It is better to make quick, decisive decisions than to deliberate for so long that it becomes paralysis by analysis. In business, one truism is clear: the big don't always eat the small, but the fast almost always eat the slow. There were a few times in my career where I made a decision to make a job change, even though I was comfortable in my current role.

I started my career as an Operations Manager for Xerox Business Services in January 1992. After several years of working hard to establish myself, I was approached about getting into a sales role. I didn't think that was for me, as I wasn't a naturally outgoing person, especially around people I didn't already know. Additionally, salespeople had an unpredictable income, and the guaranteed salary of a Sales Representative for Xerox (not including commissions) in 1997 was less than my salary as an Operations Manager.

That said, I sized up the other salespeople in our office (a talented group by the way), and determined three things to be absolute facts. First, none of them were working any harder than I was, and some of them weren't working as hard. Second, none of them were any smarter than I was. And third, on average, the sales representatives in our office were making a lot more money than I was. If the salespeople in our office weren't working any harder than I was and weren't any smarter, then it seemed to me I could make just as much money as they were. Why not?

I had to be approached several times before I finally agreed to make the change from Operations Manager to Sales Representative. But ultimately, I wasn't afraid to try something new. The real lesson here was don't be afraid to bet on yourself. To make a long story short, at the time of this writing, I have qualified for my company's President's Club award nine times in my sales career and counting. So, moving to a sales role was not all that risky, after all.

Another example of making a major decision included geography. In 1999 a Sales Manager role became available at Xerox. By 1999 I had accumulated five years of management experience, had obtained my MBA by going to school at nights at Indiana University's Kelly School of Business in an Executive program in downtown Indianapolis, and had now qualified for President's Club in two out of my first three years in sales. It seemed like a no-brainer to throw my name in the hat. I had demonstrable sales and managerial skills by this point in my career.

There was just one problem. The role was based in Louisville, Kentucky. I was born and raised in Indianapolis and had no desire to leave my hometown. Many of my high school and college friends lived in or around Indianapolis, and most of my family lived there too. While Indianapolis and Louisville are only a two-hour car drive away, this seemed like worlds apart to me at the time. This was a major decision for me. I wanted the job but did not want to move.

After a lot of thought and talking to a number of people who I respected and admired, I ultimately took the Sales Manager job in Louisville. I was young and single and could certainly move back at some point if I chose to. Also, this was clearly the logical next step in my career and professional development. This story did, in fact, have a happy ending. One year to the day after I moved down there, I met the woman who would later become my wife (Wendi Schmetzer). Needless to say, that decision turned out to be a pretty good one too.

I'll give you one more example of not being afraid to make a decision. After nine years of working for Xerox, a company I fully expected to work for my entire career, I began to have some concerns about Xerox after a large scale, botched reorganization in 2000. As the age of the internet was maturing with gale-force winds, I was also a little concerned about the ability of Xerox to adapt to this new reality. This was not a subtle or evolutionary change, but rather a secular shift in how business would be conducted moving forward.

About that same time, I began to be recruited by a company named EMC Corporation. I had heard of EMC, as I read quite often on movers and shakers in my industry, as well as high-growth companies that might be worth a few investment dollars. EMC was in the data storage business, a business that was booming due to the popularity and growth of the internet (this was circa 1999–2000). In fact, EMC was the second highest performing stock in the 1990s.

As I looked at overall business trends, one of which was the digitization of business processes and the movement from paper to digital storage, this was too good of an opportunity to ignore. Would Xerox be relevant in five years? Who was likely to be the more dynamic company moving forward, Xerox or EMC? My head said EMC, but after nine mostly good years, my heart was telling me to stick with Xerox. Additionally, a move to EMC was a very technical sale, and very different from anything I had done up to that point. Fear and doubt began to creep in. Was I smart enough to excel in a highly technical sale? Could I keep up with a fast-growing internet age company after nine years with Xerox? Would the culture be a fit for me? Would I like it? Did I really want to start over? I'd be leaving an environment where I was well established and highly thought of and moving to an environment where nobody knew me. What if things didn't work out?

Lastly, the position at EMC was that of a Sales Representative, or in other words, an individual contributor role. I had worked very hard to get into a sales leadership role at Xerox. Did I really want to go from a Manager to a Sales Representative? On the surface, this would be taking a step backward, at least from a hierarchical and responsibility standpoint.

Ultimately, I accepted a sales position with EMC in November 2000. This move turned out well. While I took a step backward in terms of responsibility, I took a major step forward in terms of income and technical knowledge. Specific to income, I had a career year in earnings my first year at EMC, by a lot. Regarding learning, I learned more about technology in my first year at EMC than I had in my previous five years at Xerox. My ride at EMC has been thrilling and rewarding.

When it comes to making difficult decisions, take the time to think things through. One good way to do this is to use a *T-chart*, something Ben Franklin used to do. A T-chart is exactly that; you put a T on a piece of paper. List the pros on one side and the cons on the other side. Laying things out like this gives you a good visual of all the different angles of a decision. And, once you have your thoughts organized in this manner, you can begin to take emotion out of your thought process and make a fact-based decision.

(3) Don't be Afraid to Fail

As you get older, and you start to think back about opportunities, things you did, things you didn't do, you will regret the things you didn't do or try far more than the things you did. What holds most people back from trying new things or taking chances is the fear of failure.

Failure is neither fatal nor final. Whatever your field of endeavor, you will have setbacks, failures, and times when things just don't seem to be going your way. In some cases, these setbacks are of no fault of your own. A few examples:

- Maybe you haven't gotten a pay raise in three straight years because the economy is doing poorly
- Maybe you lost a sale because your company had an unexpected product quality problem

- Maybe you are on a sports team, and one of your teammates committed several errors, causing your team to lose

The point is there will be setbacks in life. Use these temporary setbacks that failure brings as a learning opportunity to get better. I would submit to you that if you aren't failing periodically, then you're playing it too safe, not trying hard enough, and not stretching yourself far enough. Tommy Lasorda, the long-time manager of the Los Angeles Dodgers, had a great line on this. He said, "Pressure is a word that is misused in our vocabulary. When you start thinking of pressure, it's because you've started to think of failure." If you're not afraid to fail, then pressure becomes your ally. If you are afraid of failure, then pressure will paralyze you. Your mental attitude will determine whether pressure is your friend or foe, and you can choose which one it will be. A little pressure is a good thing. It sharpens your focus, gets your blood pumping, and brings out 100 percent effort in whatever it is that you're doing.

I'll give you two examples from my past regarding failure, one positive and one negative.

In 2003 I changed sales roles with EMC. I moved from what is called a farmer, where you have mostly existing clients, to a role of a hunter, one in which you are mostly cold-calling in an attempt to open new accounts. I had never really cold-called in my sales career up to that point and didn't really know how to go about it. True to my nature, I purchased a couple of books on how to prospect and how to cold-call. For anyone that has cold-called, this can be a nerve-racking task. Many salespeople don't make calls because they fear rejection. I looked at this as the opposite. Cold-calling wasn't something to fear, but it was instead an opportunity. Every call I made got me one step closer to a sale. And since I was calling by phone, what was the worst thing that could happen? They hang up, and I go on about my day. That doesn't seem so harsh.

By the end of 2003, I had taken the mid-market business in Kentucky from one installed account to 14 and qualified for President's Club. Not bad for a novice cold-caller. I'm convinced my attitude toward this new role had more to do with my success than anything else.

A second example is one in which I was afraid to fail, which led to inaction. I mentioned my hesitation in pursuing a sales career at Xerox earlier. It took three years for me to muster up the courage to try something outside my comfort zone. As I look back, that three-year delay in getting into a more lucrative sales role, by my best estimate, cost me approximately $250,000 in incremental income. Had I invested that money at an average annual return of just 5% and left it alone, that nut would now be worth in the neighborhood of $550,000. *Sometimes the riskiest thing you can do is to do nothing. Conversely, sometimes the safest thing you can do is to get out there and try new things, make things happen, and bet on yourself.* While trying new things, you need to make educated, calculated decisions. But every once in a while, you need to get outside your comfort zone in order to grow. I'm certainly not recommending you haphazardly bounce from one thing to the next. But, as the professional golfer John Daly used to say, "Grip it and rip it." There is a time and place for this mentality and approach.

(4) Don't be Afraid to Laugh at Yourself

It is important to take your career seriously, but not yourself. Life can be stressful, and one of the best ways to combat stress is to laugh. Sometimes we screw up, and people laugh at us. Oftentimes people get defensive and fire back at people who are laughing at them. Don't be afraid to laugh at yourself, maybe even poke fun at yourself. You will earn a lot of points with people when you can laugh off your own mistakes or shortcomings. And a side benefit is you will let off some steam and minimize stress at the same time. A little humility never hurt anyone.

Bob Uecker was a great example of this. Bob Uecker was a Major League baseball player. By any standards, he was a marginal ballplayer. He was a catcher who spent six years in the Majors and had a career batting average of .200. His sense of humor, quick wit, and ability to make fun of himself led to a very successful broadcasting career. In fact, the famous night time television host, Johnny Carson, once called Bob the funniest man he had ever met; high praise coming from a man who made a living in comedy. Johnny Carson thought so much of Bob that he had him as a guest on his show approximately one hundred times.

To illustrate his quick wit and ability to poke fun at himself, Bob was announcing a Monday Night Baseball game with two other famous people, Al Michaels and Howard Cosell. During the game, Howard Cosell had suggested a particular situation in the game called for a bunt. Bob disagreed, and went on to explain to Cosell and the viewing audience why a bunt, at that particular time, was not the best course of action. Cosell reluctantly agreed, saying, "Well, Ukie, you have a point. But, did you have to be so truculent about it. You do know what truculent means, don't you?" Without missing a beat, Bob replied, "Of course, Howard. If you had a truck, and I borrowed it, that would be a truck-you-lent." Rather than get upset or defensive over not knowing the definition of a word, or try to play it off that he knew something he didn't, he poked fun at himself instead. And, he did it without degrading Cosell in the process. *Beautiful.*

(5) Don't Assume

Assume can be spelled ASS-U-ME. When you assume, you make an ass out of you and me, as the saying goes. Making wrong assumptions is costly, both in terms of time and money. And, we can make ourselves look foolish with wrong assumptions. To illustrate, one of my favorite movie series is the *Pink Panther* movies, which were comedies written by Blake Edwards and starring the late Peter Sellers. Peter Sellers played Inspector Jacques Clouseau, a bumbling idiot of a detective who consistently seemed to get lucky in solving crimes despite his clumsy, incompetent, and hilarious methods. In one movie, he was checking into a hotel, and there was a dog sitting in the lobby. The scene went like this:

Inspector Clouseau: "Does your dog bite?" he said to the bellman behind the desk.
Bellman: "No," he replied.

Inspector Clouseau: He bent down to pet the dog, and the dog bit him. Clouseau said, "I thought you said your dog does not bite."
Bellman: "That is not my dog."

Take the time to get the facts, because things are not always as they seem.

(6) Don't Be Afraid to Go Against the Grain

One final thought that relates to this topic is don't be afraid of your own value systems. When I was in seventh grade, a friend of mine that I played sports with was making fun of one of the kids in school. This kid's name was Shawn (fictitious). He was shy, overweight, and didn't appear to have many friends. After a few weeks of listening to my friend relentlessly make fun of Shawn's weight during our first-period class, I finally stepped in and told my friend to leave him alone. My friend ultimately did. I felt good about being able to help this kid out, who didn't deserve to be made fun of. Nobody deserves to be made fun of just because they are a little different.

That said, I read in our local newspaper that following summer that Shawn was killed in a tragic tractor accident on a farm near Brownsburg.

I felt horrible and thought of Shawn a lot over the years. It must have been torture to come to school every day knowing you were going to get picked on and made fun of. I personally felt a little ashamed, ashamed I hadn't stepped in a lot sooner to help. The moral of the story is to follow your value systems. And, if you can help someone out along the way, do it. That is precisely what leaders do. Leaders do what is right, not necessarily what is popular.

(7) Don't EVER be afraid to Be Yourself

Be yourself, and don't be afraid to speak up. Voice your opinion. Many people keep quiet because they are afraid they might offend someone. That someone is no more important than you are. If you state something politely, and honestly, who cares if they don't like it? *Be who you want to be, and say what you want to say.* People who mind don't matter, and people who matter don't mind.

There is a poem that I heard Bill Parcells, Hall of Fame football coach, recite once during an interview that addresses this point better than anything else I could possibly say.

The Guy in the Glass

When you get what you want in your struggle for pelf
And the world makes you King for a day,
Then go to the mirror and look at yourself,
And see what that guy has to say.

For it isn't your Father, or Mother, or Wife,
Who judgement upon you must pass.
The feller whose verdict counts most in your life
Is the guy staring back from the glass.

He's the feller to please, never mind all the rest,
For he's with you clear up to the end,
And you've passed your most dangerous, difficult test
If the guy in the glass is your friend.

A Collection of Thoughts

You may be like Jack Horner and "chisel" a plum,
And think you're a wonderful guy,
But the man in the glass says you're only a bum
If you can't look him straight in the eye.

You can fool the whole world down the pathway of years,
And get pats on your back as you pass,
But your final reward will be heartaches and tears
If you've cheated the guy in the glass.

By Peter "Dale" Wimbrow Sr.

Final Thoughts

Hopefully, this book is a resource you can turn to for guidance if and when I'm not around to help. If you can consistently do the following six things, I promise you that will be more than good enough as you go through life.

- **Always give your very best**, no matter what the task.

- **Always follow the Golden Rule** and treat others as you would have them treat you. People will forget what you said. They may forget what you did. They will never forget how you made them feel.

- **Always be honest** for it truly is the best policy. Lying makes a mistake a part of your future. Telling the truth makes the mistake a part of your past.

- **Always do what you say you're going to do** and be a person that can be counted on.

- **Always be working toward inspiring goals** that cause you to stretch, to be better than your previous self.

- **Always follow the Ten Commandments:**

  1. I am the Lord, your God.
  2. Thou shall bring no false idols before me.
  3. Do not take the name of the Lord in vain.
  4. Remember the Sabbath and keep it holy.

5. Honor thy father and thy mother.

6. Thou shall not kill.

7. Thou shall not commit adultery.

8. Thou shall not steal.

9. Thou shall not bear false witness against your neighbor.

10. Thou shall not covet your neighbor's wife (or anything that belongs to your neighbor).

Throughout my life, I've been a number of things: son, brother, cousin, student, friend, athlete, production supervisor, sales representative, uncle, husband, district manager, regional vice president, just to name a few. The one thing I'm the most proud of, the most humbled by, is being your Dad. It's an awesome responsibility, but it's also an awesome honor and privilege.

Be proud of yourself and where you came from, and enjoy the journey along the way. It's been my experience people are about as happy as they make up their minds to be. Put another way, *life is mostly what you make of it, so make it what you want. You can have, be, or do anything you want in life.* The only variable is time. And you have full control over your time. Are you spending it or investing it? The choice is yours.

- You have a choice on how you spend your time.

- You have a choice on what thoughts you allow to occupy your mind.

- You have a choice on who you spend your time with.

- You have a choice on what your chosen career is.

- You have a choice on who you marry.

- You have a choice on what kind of attitude you have when you awake in the morning (positive or negative, hopeful or depressed).

- You have a choice on what goals to pursue.

- You have a choice on how you treat others.

- You have a choice on whether to live a healthy lifestyle.

- You have a choice on how determined you are.

- You have a choice on how hard you work.

Always remember, you have a choice!!

Since the day each one of you was born, I've said a little prayer every night as I lay my head down to sleep. "Please, God, keep my family happy, healthy, and safe, all the days of their lives." If God answers this one simple prayer, I will truly rest in peace.

Good luck Nicholas, Hayli Rose, and Noah. I will be with you every step of the way, physically and in spirit.

I Love You.

Your Biggest Fan,

Dad

APPENDIX

A

MISCELLANEOUS QUOTES

"Courage is being scared to death, but saddling up anyway."
  – Unknown

"Mental is to physical as 4 is to 1."
  Bob Knight, Retired Hall of Fame College Basketball Coach

"It is the nature of man to rise to greatness if greatness is expected of him."
  – Unknown

"To see what is right and not do it is a lack of courage."
  – Confucius, Philosopher

"People who attempt the difficult often attain the impossible."
  – Unknown

"Confidence is the most important single factor in this game. And no matter how great your natural talent, there is only one way to obtain and sustain it – WORK."
  – Jack Nicklaus, Professional Golfer

"If you don't design your own life plan, chances are you'll fall into someone else's."
  – Unknown

"If you will do what most people won't do for a few years, then you can do what most people can't do for the rest of your life."
  – Chuck Sumpter, Network Marketer

A Collection of Thoughts

"Few men during their lifetime come anywhere near exhausting the resources dwelling within them. There are deep wells of strength and intelligence that are never used."
– Unknown

"Age wrinkles the body. Quitting wrinkles the soul."
– Bob Proctor, Motivational Speaker and Author

"The highest reward for a man's toil is not what he gets for it but what he becomes by it."
– Unknown

"A man flattened by an opponent can get up again. A man flattened by conformity stays down for good."
– Unknown

"Consult not your fears, but your hopes and dreams. Think not about your frustrations, but about your unfulfilled potential. Concern yourself not with what you have tried and failed in, but with what is still possible for you to do."
– Unknown

"Those of you who think you know it all are very annoying to those of us who do."
– Doug Huse, the late, great High School Basketball Coach

"He who truly knows has no occasion to shout."
– Unknown

"There are a thousand excuses for failure but never a good reason."
– Mark Twain, Author and Satirist

"No great performance ever came from holding back."
– Unknown

"Ambition is the path to success. Persistence is the vehicle you arrive in."
– Unknown

"In a time of drastic change, it is the learners who inherit the future."
– Unknown

"Success is the ability to go from failure to failure without losing your enthusiasm."
  – Unknown

"Don't judge each day by the harvest you reap but by the seeds you plant."
  – Unknown

"The majority of men meet with failure because of their lack of persistence in creating new plans to take the place of those that failed."
  – Unknown

"We are what we repeatedly do. Excellence is therefore not an act, but a habit."
  – Aristotle, Philosopher

"Courage must come from the soul within; the man must furnish the will to win. So figure it out for yourself, my lad; you were born with all that the great have had."
  – Edgar Guest, Poet

"You are today where the thoughts of yesterday have brought you. And you will be tomorrow where the thoughts of today take you."
  – Unknown

"Fix the problem, not the blame."
  – Japanese Proverb

"The discipline of writing something down is the first step toward making it happen."
  – Lee Iacocca, Business Executive

"It's what you do after you do what you're expected to do that counts."
  – Brian Tracy, Author

"Men are not prisoners of fate, but only prisoners of their own minds."
  – Franklin Delano Roosevelt, President of the United States of America

"Always make a total effort, even when the odds are against you."
  – Arnold Palmer, Professional Golfer

"The secret of success in life is for a person to be ready for opportunity when it comes."
> – Benjamin Disraeli, British Politician

"You are younger today than you will ever be again. Make use of it for the sake of tomorrow."
> – Norman Cousins, Editor and Writer

"When one door closes, another door opens. But we often look so long and so regretfully upon the closed door that we do not see the ones which open for us."
> – Alexander Graham Bell, Inventor

"The two most powerful warriors are patience and time."
> – Leo Tolstoy, Author

"The real voyage of discovery consists not in seeking new landscapes, but in having new eyes."
> – Marcel Proust, Author

"We are always complaining that our days are few, and acting as though there would be no end to them."
> – Lucius Amnaeus Seneca, Philosopher

"In reading the lives of great men, I found that the first victory they won was over themselves. Self-discipline with all of them came first."
> – Harry Truman, 33rd President of the United States

"Do you love life? Then do not squander time, for that's the stuff life is made of."
> – Benjamin Franklin, Inventor

"Perpetual optimism is a force multiplier."
> – Colin Powell, US Soldier and Diplomat

"Concentrate all your thoughts on the task at hand. The sun's rays do not burn until brought to a focus."
> – Alexander Graham Bell, Inventor

"Obstacles are those frightful things you see when you take your eyes off the goal."
> – Henry Ford, Founder of the Ford Motor Company

"Every man dies. Not every man lives. The only limits to the possibilities in your life tomorrow are the 'buts' you use today."
  – Les Brown, Bandleader

"Your own resolution to succeed is more important than any other one thing."
  – Abraham Lincoln, 16th President of the United States

"The greatest danger for most of us is not that our aim is too high and we miss it, but that it is too low and we reach it."
  – Michelangelo, Artist

"Don't let yesterday take up too much of today."
  – Will Rogers, Actor

"People of mediocre ability sometimes achieve outstanding success because they don't know when to quit. Most men succeed because they are determined to."
  – George Allen, Football Coach

"Discipline is the bridge between goals and accomplishment."
  – Jim Rohn, Author

"Energy and persistence conquer all things."
  – Benjamin Franklin, Inventor and US Diplomat

"The happiest people in the world are those who feel absolutely terrific about themselves, and this is the natural outgrowth of accepting total responsibility for every part of your life."
  – Brian Tracy, Author

"You can only get ahead with your desired lifestyle if you are focused on the things that will produce that lifestyle."
  – Jack Canfield, Success Coach

"In the confrontation between the stream and the rock, the stream always wins, not through strength but by perseverance."
  – H. Jackson Brown, Actor

"How am I going to live today in order to create the tomorrow I'm committed to?"
  – Anthony Robbins, Motivational Speaker

A Collection of Thoughts

"Goals provide the energy source that powers our lives. One of the best ways we can get the most from the energy we have is to focus it. That is what goals can do for us: concentrate our energy."
– Dennis Waitley, Motivational Speaker and Writer

"Control your own destiny or someone else will."
– Jack Welch, Business Executive and Writer

"It is not the strongest of the species that survive, nor the most intelligent, but the one most responsive to change."
– Charles Darwin, Geologist and Biologist

"Don't let what you can't do interfere with what you can do."
– John Wooden, Basketball Coach

"A clear vision, backed by definite plans, gives you a tremendous feeling of confidence and personal power."
– Brian Tracy, Author

"Character is much easier kept than recovered."
– Thomas Paine, Author

"I've found that luck is quite predictable. If you want more luck, take more chances. Be more active. Show up more often."
– Brian Tracy, Author

"There are only two options regarding commitment. You're either in or out. There is no such thing as a life in between."
– Pat Riley, NBA Basketball Coach and Player

"Your attitude, not your aptitude, will determine your altitude."
– Zig Ziglar, Author

"Fear melts when you take action towards a goal you really want."
– Robert G. Allen, Author

"Formulate and stamp indelibly on your mind a mental picture of yourself as succeeding. Hold this picture tenaciously. Never permit it to fade. Your mind will seek to develop the picture."
– Norman Vincent Peale, Author

"If you go to work on your goals, your goals will go to work on you. If you go to work on your plan, your plan will go to work on you. Whatever good things we build, end up building us."
    – Jim Rohn, Motivational Speaker and Author

"20 years from now you will be more disappointed by the things that you didn't do than by the things that you did. So throw off the bowlines. Sail away from the safe harbor. Catch the trade winds in your sails. Explore. Dream. Discover."
    – Mark Twain, Author

"Effort, not ability, makes the biggest difference in achievement."
    – Bill Clinton, 42nd President of the United States

"Chance favors the prepared mind."
    – Louis Pasteur, Chemist

"Victory favors the team that makes the fewest mistakes."
    – Bob Knight, College Basketball Coach

"The man who can drive himself further once the effort gets painful is the man who will win."
    – Roger Bannister, Runner

"Many of us spend half our time wishing for things we could have if we didn't spend half our time wishing."
    – Alexander Woolcott, Critic and Writer

"Fix your eyes forward on what you can change, not back on what you cannot change."
    – Tom Clancy, Author

"Cherish your visions and your dreams, as they are the children of your soul, the blueprints of your ultimate achievement."
    – Napoleon Hill, Pioneer of Personal Achievement Philosophy
      and Author

"Go confidently in the direction of your dreams. Live the life you have imagined."
    – Henry David Thoreau, Author

"If we did all the things we are capable of, we would literally astonish ourselves."
  – Thomas Edison, Inventor

"Nurture your mind with great thoughts for you will never go any higher than you think."
  – Benjamin Disraeli, 1st Earl of Beaconsfield

"One's only security in life comes from doing something uncommonly well."
  – Abraham Lincoln, 16th President of the United States

"People with goals succeed because they know where they are going."
  – Earl Nightingale, Motivational Speaker

"No amount of talent or ability is sufficient if it's not backed by:
• An extraordinary work ethic
• A positive attitude
• Uplifting goals
• A commitment to continuous learning"
  – Mike Johns, Author and Businessman

"Four short words sum up what has lifted most successful individuals above the crowd: a little bit more. They did all that was expected of them and a little bit more."
  – Lou Vickery, American Business Writer

"Once you surrender to your vision, success begins to chase you."
  – Unknown

"Be not afraid of going slowly. Be only afraid of standing still."
  – Chinese Proverb

"You must have long-term goals to keep you from getting frustrated by short-term failures."
  – Charles C. Noble, Major General and Engineer

"We must develop and maintain the capacity to forgive. He who is devoid of the power to forgive is devoid of the power to love."
  – Martin Luther King Jr., Minister and Activist

"*Successful people form the habit of doing what failures don't like to do. They like the results they get by doing what they don't necessarily enjoy.*"
   – Earl Nightingale, Motivational Speaker

"*Gauge your success by what you gave up to achieve it.*"
   – Eden Hampson

"*If opportunity doesn't knock, build a door.*"
   – Milton Berlet

"*Let me tell you the secret that has led to my goal. My strength lies solely in my tenacity.*"
   – Louis Pasteur, Chemist and Microbiologist

"*Create the highest, grandest vision possible for your life, because you become what you believe.*"
   – Oprah Winfrey, Talk Show Host

"80% of what is standing between where you are today and where you want to be is within you."
   – Brian Tracy, Author

"*I am willing to put myself through anything; temporary pain or discomfort means nothing to me as long as I can see that the experience will take me to a new level.*"
   – Diana Nyad, Swimmer

"*Fear of failure and fear of the unknown are always defeated by faith. Having faith in yourself, in the process of change, and in the new direction that change sets will reveal your own inner strength.*"
   – Georgette Mosbacher, Business Executive

"*It takes courage to grow up to be who you really are.*"
   – E. E. Cummings

"*Lord grant me the serenity to accept the things I cannot change, the power to change the things I can, and the wisdom to know the difference.*"
   – Alcoholics Anonymous Serenity Prayer

"*Life is 10% what happens to me and 90% how I choose to react to it.*"
   – Charles Swindoll, Pastor and Author

A Collection of Thoughts

"If you are distressed by anything external, the pain is not due to the thing itself but to your estimate of it; and this you have the power to revoke at any moment."
— Marcus Aurelius, Roman Emperor and Stoic Philosopher

"Change is the law of life and those who look only to the past or present are certain to miss the future."
— John F. Kennedy, 35th President of the United States

"The best thing you can do is get very good at being you."
— Dennis the Menace

"Good judgment comes from experience. Unfortunately, experience sometimes comes from bad judgment."
— Mike Johns, Author and Businessman

"The will to win is not nearly as important as the will to prepare to win."
— Bob Knight, Hall of Fame College Basketball Coach

"Adversity doesn't make character, rather it reveals it."
— Unknown

"In striving for continuous improvement, don't be afraid to get worse in order to get better."
— Tiger Woods, Professional Golfer

"If you aren't fired with enthusiasm, you will be fired with enthusiasm."
— Vince Lombardi, American Football Coach

"In a moment of decision the best thing you can do is the right thing. The worst thing you can do is nothing."
— Theodore Roosevelt, 26th President of the United States

"Obstacles cannot crush me; every obstacle yields to stern resolve."
— Leonardo Da Vinci, Painter, Sculptor, and Architect

"The chains of habit are too weak to be felt until they are too strong to be broken."
— Samuel Johnson, Lexicographer

"People who say that life is not worthwhile are really saying that they themselves have no personal goals which are worthwhile ... Get yourself a goal worth working for. Better still, get yourself a project ... Always have something ahead of you to 'look forward to' – work for and hope for."
   – Maxwell Maltz, Physician and Author

"In the absence of clearly-defined goals, we become strangely loyal to performing daily trivia until ultimately we become enslaved by it."
   – Robert Heinlein, American Novelist

"Self-image sets the boundaries of accomplishment."
   – Maxwell Maltz, Physician and Author

"Lost time is never found again."
   – Benjamin Franklin, Inventor

"What this power is, I cannot say. All I know is that it exists...and it becomes available only when you are in the state of mind in which you know exactly what you want...and are fully determined not to quit until you get it."
   – Alexander Graham Bell, Inventor and Educator

"The first great gift we can bestow on others is a good example."
   – Thomas Morell, Librettist

"Whatever you want to do, do it now. There are only so many tomorrows."
   – Michael Landon, Actor

"It's better to look ahead and prepare than to look back and regret."
   – Jacki Joyner-Kersee, Athlete

"The happiness of most people we know is not ruined by great catastrophes or fatal errors, but by the repetition of slowly destructive little things."
   – Ernest Dimnet, French Priest and Writer

"Set your sights high, the higher the better. Expect the most wonderful things to happen, not in the future but right now. Realize that nothing is too good. Allow absolutely nothing to hamper you or hold you up in any way."
   – Eileen Caddy, Author

A Collection of Thoughts

"Our attitude toward life determines life's attitude towards us."
– Earl Nightingale, Author of The Strangest Secret

"Nothing great has ever been achieved except by those who dared believe that something inside them was superior to circumstances."
– Bruce Barton, Advertising Executive

"You are the master of your life, you are the master of your mind, you have the power to change the way you think and feel. You have the power in you to achieve your goals, to become the person you want to be, and to live the life of your dreams."
– Zlatoslava Petrak, Author of Open To The Infinite Riches Of The Universe

"If you want more, you have to require more from yourself."
– Dr. Phil, Motivational Author and Talk Show Host

"Fix your eyes forward on what you can do, not back on what you cannot change."
– Tom Clancy, Author

"When you believe and think 'I can,' you activate your motivation, commitment, confidence, concentration and excitement – all of which relate directly to achievement."
– Dr. Jerry Lynch

"Focus more on your desire than on your doubt, and the dream will take care of itself. You may be surprised at how easily this happens. Your doubts are not as powerful as your desires, unless you make them so."
– Marcia Wieder, Speaker and Author

"Only those who risk going too far can possibly find out how far one can go."
– T.S. Eliot, Author

"Until you commit your goals to paper, you have intentions that are seeds without soil."
– Anonymous

"The important thing is to learn a lesson every time you lose."
– John McEnroe, Tennis Champion

"The moment you commit and quit holding back, all sorts of unforeseen incidents, meetings and material assistance, will rise up to help you. The simple act of commitment is a powerful magnet for help."
    – Napoleon Hill, Pioneer of Personal Achievement Philosophy and Author

"The principle is competing against yourself. It's about self-improvement, about being better than you were the day before."
    – Steve Young, Football Player

"It comes from saying no to 1,000 things to make sure we don't get on the wrong track or try to do too much. We're always thinking about new markets we could enter, but it's only by saying no that you can concentrate on the things that are really important."
    – Steve Jobs, Apple Co-founder

"Don't wait for extraordinary opportunities. Seize common occasions and make them great. Weak men wait for opportunities; strong men make them."
    – Orison Swett Marden, Author

"Character is the ability to carry out a good resolution long after the excitement of the moment has passed."
    – Cavett Robert, Motivational Speaker

"Talent is cheaper than table salt. What separates the talented individual from the successful one is a lot of hard work."
    – Stephen King, Author

"There is no passion to be found playing small, in settling for a life that is less than the one you are capable of living."
    – Nelson Mandela, 11th President of South Africa

"Do more than is required. What is the distance between someone who achieves their goals consistently and those who spend their lives and careers merely following? The extra mile."
    – Gary Ryan Blair, Author and Motivational Speaker

"The grateful mind is constantly fixed upon the best. Therefore it tends to become the best. It takes the form of character of the best, and will receive the best."
    – Wallace D. Wattles, Author of The Science of Getting Rich

A Collection of Thoughts

"The more you take responsibility for your past and present, the more you are able to create the future you seek."
  – Celestine Chua, Author and Blogger

"Don't play for safety. It's the most dangerous thing in the world."
  – Hugh Walpole, Writer

"What you lack in talent can be made up with desire, hustle and giving 110% all the time."
  – Don Zimmer, Baseball Manager

"To sit back and let fate play its hand out and never influence it is not the way man was meant to operate."
  – John Glenn, astronaut

"As long as you're going to be thinking anyway, think big."
  – Donald Trump, Real Estate Magnate

"You gain strength, courage, and confidence by every experience in which you really stop to look fear in the face. You are able to say to yourself, 'I have lived through this horror. I can take the next thing that comes along.'…You must do the thing you think you cannot do."
  – Eleanor Roosevelt, Former First Lady

"Good character is more to be praised than outstanding talent. Most talents are, to some extent, a gift. Good character, by contrast, is not given to us. We have to build it, piece by piece – by thought, by choice, courage, and determination."
  – Coach Matt Labrum

"The most important thing is your self-respect. It doesn't matter what people think about you, but what you think about yourself."
  – Robert H. Abplanalp, Inventor and Engineer

"Your life is a print-out of your thoughts."
  – Steve Maraboli, Author and Speaker

"If you don't change your beliefs, your life will be like this forever. Is that good news?"
  – Douglas Adams, Writer and Humorist

"More gold has been mined from the thoughts of man than has been taken from the earth."
  – Napoleon Hill, Pioneer of Personal Achievement Philosophy and Author

"There are no traffic jams on the extra mile."
  – Roger Staubach, Retired NFL Quarterback

"Success in any endeavor does not happen by accident. Rather, it's the result of deliberate decisions, conscious effort, and immense persistence … all directed at specific goals."
  – Gary Ryan Blair, Author and Motivational Speaker

"A vision is a clearly articulated, results-oriented picture of a future you intend to create. It is a dream with direction."
  – Jesse Stoner Zemel, Author

"When you let me take, I'm grateful. When you let me give, I'm blessed."
  – Leonard Nimoy, Actor and Director

"Education is of no value and talent is worthless – unless you have an unwavering aim. Never find yourself without a compass."
  – Condoleezza Rice, Secretary of State

"I do not feel obliged to believe that the same God who has endowed us with sense, reason, and intellect has intended us to forgo their use."
  – Galileo Galilei, Astronomer

"Reality can destroy the dream; why shouldn't the dream destroy the reality?"
  – George More, Novelist

APPENDIX

RECOMMENDED BOOKS

Over the years, I have been a voracious reader, always looking for new ideas on how I could become more effective in my career.

Below are a few books I have read over the years on motivation and self-improvement. I hope you find these books helpful.

Goal Setting:

Goals – Brian Tracy

Flight Plan – Brian Tracy

Focal Point – Brian Tracy

Lead the Field – Earl Nightingale

The Strangest Secret – Earl Nightingale

Motivational:

You Were Born Rich – Bob Proctor

Success is a Choice – Rick Pitino

Rebound Rules – Rick Pitino

Think and Grow Rich – Napoleon Hill

The Secret – Rhonda Byrne

The Magic of Thinking Big – Dr. David J. Schwartz

The Magic of Thinking Success – Dr. David J. Schwartz

The Answer – John Assaraf & Murray Smith

A Collection of Thoughts

Failing Forward – John C. Maxwell

Napoleon Hill's A Year of Growing Rich – Napoleon Hill

The Success Principle – Jack Canfield

Your Infinite Power To Be Rich – Joseph Murphy

You2 – Price Pritchett

Sales:

Cold-Calling Techniques – Stephan Schiffman

Selling to VITO – Tony Parinello

Let's Get Real or Let's Not Play – Mahan Khalsa

You Can't Teach a Kid to Ride a Bike at a Seminar – David Sandler

SPIN Selling – Neil Rackham

How I Raised Myself From Failure to Success in Selling – Frank Bettger

Secrets of Question Based Selling – Thomas A. Freese

Leadership/Management:

Lincoln on Leadership – Donald T. Phillips

The 21 Irrefutable Laws of Leadership – John C. Maxwell

The Leadership Challenge – James M. Kouzes & Barry Z. Posner

Winning – Jack Welch

Jack: Straight From the Gut – Jack Welch

Wins, Losses, and Lessons – Lou Holtz

Winning Every Day – Lou Holtz

The 7 Habits of Highly Effective People – Stephen R. Covey

The Genius of Sitting Bull – Emmet C. Murphy

The Leadership Secrets of Attila the Hun – Wess Roberts

The 21 Most Powerful Minutes in a Leader's Day – John C. Maxwell

Developing the Leader within You – John C. Maxwell

Developing the Leaders Around You – John C. Maxwell

Finances:

Safe Money Millionaire – Brett Kitchen and Ethan Kap

Rich Dad's Retire Young Retire Rich – Robert Kyosaki

Rich Dad's Cashflow Quadrant – Robert Kyosaki

The Millionaire Next Door – Thomas J. Stanley & William D. Danko

Multiple Streams of Income – Robert G. Allen

The Warren Buffet Way – Robert G. Hagstrom

The Intelligent Investor – Benjamin Graham

Security Analysis – Benjamin Graham

Financial Self Defense – Charles Givens

APPENDIX

IRISH PROVERB

May we all feel

happy and contented,

healthy and strong,

safe and protected

and living with ease.

~

May the road rise up to meet you.

May the wind be always at your back.

May the sun shine warm upon your face,

and rains fall soft upon your fields.

And until we meet again,

May God hold you in the palm of His hand.

APPENDIX

WHAT IT TAKES TO BE NUMBER ONE
VINCE LOMBARDI

"Winning is not a sometime thing; it's an all the time thing. You don't win once in a while; you don't do things right once in a while; you do them right all of the time. Winning is a habit. Unfortunately, so is losing.

There is no room for second place. There is only one place in my game, and that's first place. I have finished second twice in my time at Green Bay, and I don't ever want to finish second again. There is a second place bowl game, but it is a game for losers played by losers. It is and always has been an American zeal to be first in anything we do, and to win, and to win, and to win.

Every time a football player goes to ply his trade he's got to play from the ground up - from the soles of his feet right up to his head. Every inch of him has to play. Some guys play with their heads. That's OK. You've got to be smart to be number one in any business. But more importantly, you've got to play with your heart, with every fiber of your body. If you're lucky enough to find a guy with a lot of head and a lot of heart, he's never going to come off the field second.

Running a football team is no different than running any other kind of organization—an army, a political party or a business. The principles are the same. The object is to win—to beat the other guy. Maybe that sounds hard or cruel. I don't think it is.

A Collection of Thoughts

It is a reality of life that men are competitive and the most competitive games draw the most competitive men. That's why they are there—to compete. The object is to win fairly, squarely, by the rules—but to win.

And in truth, I've never known a man worth his salt who in the long run, deep down in his heart, didn't appreciate the grind, the discipline. There is something in good men that really yearns for discipline and the harsh reality of head to head combat.

I don't say these things because I believe in the 'brute' nature of men or that men must be brutalized to be combative. I believe in God, and I believe in human decency. But I firmly believe that any man's finest hour—his greatest fulfillment to all he holds dear—is that moment when he has worked his heart out in a good cause and lies exhausted on the field of battle—victorious."

By Coach Vincent T. Lombardi

APPENDIX

AMORTIZATION SCHEDULES

30-Year Mortgage

- Buy a $300,000 home.

- Put 20% down or $60,000.

- This leaves a $240,000 mortgage, spread over 360 equal monthly payments.

- Fixed Interest Rate is 5.0%.

- Early on, the bulk of your payment is interest. As you pay off the loan over time, the pendulum shifts to more principal than interest. Thus, it is more impactful to make extra payments early than late.

- Note the total interest paid of $223,813 at the bottom of this schedule. Thus, **the $240,000 loan actually costs you $463,813**.

PMT	PRINCIPAL	INTEREST	Total Payment	BALANCE
1	$ 288.37	$ 1,000.00	$ 1,288.37	$ 239,711.63
2	$ 289.57	$ 998.80	$ 1,288.37	$ 239,422.06
3	$ 290.78	$ 997.59	$ 1,288.37	$ 239,131.28
4	$ 291.99	$ 996.38	$ 1,288.37	$ 238,839.29
5	$ 293.21	$ 995.16	$ 1,288.37	$ 238,546.08
6	$ 294.43	$ 993.94	$ 1,288.37	$ 238,251.65
7	$ 295.65	$ 992.72	$ 1,288.37	$ 237,956.00

PMT	PRINCIPAL	INTEREST	Total Payment	BALANCE
8	$ 296.89	$ 991.48	$ 1,288.37	$ 237,659.11
9	$ 298.12	$ 990.25	$ 1,288.37	$ 237,360.99
10	$ 299.37	$ 989.00	$ 1,288.37	$ 237,061.62
11	$ 300.61	$ 987.76	$ 1,288.37	$ 236,761.01
12	$ 301.87	$ 986.50	$ 1,288.37	$ 236,459.14
13	$ 303.12	$ 985.25	$ 1,288.37	$ 236,156.02
14	$ 304.39	$ 983.98	$ 1,288.37	$ 235,851.63
15	$ 305.65	$ 982.72	$ 1,288.37	$ 235,545.98
16	$ 306.93	$ 981.44	$ 1,288.37	$ 235,239.05
17	$ 308.21	$ 980.16	$ 1,288.37	$ 234,930.84
18	$ 309.49	$ 978.88	$ 1,288.37	$ 234,621.35
19	$ 310.78	$ 977.59	$ 1,288.37	$ 234,310.57
20	$ 312.08	$ 976.29	$ 1,288.37	$ 233,998.49
21	$ 313.38	$ 974.99	$ 1,288.37	$ 233,685.11
22	$ 314.68	$ 973.69	$ 1,288.37	$ 233,370.43
23	$ 315.99	$ 972.38	$ 1,288.37	$ 233,054.44
24	$ 317.31	$ 971.06	$ 1,288.37	$ 232,737.13
25	$ 318.63	$ 969.74	$ 1,288.37	$ 232,418.50
26	$ 319.96	$ 968.41	$ 1,288.37	$ 232,098.54
27	$ 321.29	$ 967.08	$ 1,288.37	$ 231,777.25
28	$ 322.63	$ 965.74	$ 1,288.37	$ 231,454.62
29	$ 323.98	$ 964.39	$ 1,288.37	$ 231,130.64
30	$ 325.33	$ 963.04	$ 1,288.37	$ 230,805.31
31	$ 326.68	$ 961.69	$ 1,288.37	$ 230,478.63
32	$ 328.04	$ 960.33	$ 1,288.37	$ 230,150.59
33	$ 329.41	$ 958.96	1,288.37	$ 229,821.18
34	$ 330.78	$ 957.59	$ 1,288.37	$ 229,490.40
35	$ 332.16	$ 956.21	$ 1,288.37	$ 229,158.24

PMT	PRINCIPAL	INTEREST	Total Payment	BALANCE
36	$ 333.54	$ 954.83	$ 1,288.37	$ 228,824.70
37	$ 334.93	$ 953.44	$ 1,288.37	$ 228,489.77
38	$ 336.33	$ 952.04	$ 1,288.37	$ 228,153.44
39	$ 337.73	$ 950.64	$ 1,288.37	$ 227,815.71
40	$ 339.14	$ 949.23	$ 1,288.37	$ 227,476.57
41	$ 340.55	$ 947.82	$ 1,288.37	$ 227,136.02
42	$ 341.97	$ 946.40	$ 1,288.37	$ 226,794.05
43	$ 343.39	$ 944.98	$ 1,288.37	$ 226,450.66
44	$ 344.83	$ 943.54	$ 1,288.37	$ 226,105.83
45	$ 346.26	$ 942.11	$ 1,288.37	$ 225,759.57
46	$ 347.71	$ 940.66	$ 1,288.37	$ 225,411.86
47	$ 349.15	$ 939.22	$ 1,288.37	$ 225,062.71
48	$ 350.61	$ 937.76	$ 1,288.37	$ 224,712.10
49	$ 352.07	$ 936.30	$ 1,288.37	$ 224,360.03
50	$ 353.54	$ 934.83	$ 1,288.37	$ 224,006.49
51	$ 355.01	$ 933.36	$ 1,288.37	$ 223,651.48
52	$ 356.49	$ 931.88	$ 1,288.37	$ 223,294.99
53	$ 357.97	$ 930.40	$ 1,288.37	$ 222,937.02
54	$ 359.47	$ 928.90	$ 1,288.37	$ 222,577.55
55	$ 360.96	$ 927.41	$ 1,288.37	$ 222,216.59
56	$ 362.47	$ 925.90	$ 1,288.37	$ 221,854.12
57	$ 363.98	$ 924.39	$ 1,288.37	$ 221,490.14
58	$ 365.49	$ 922.88	$ 1,288.37	$ 221,124.65
59	$ 367.02	$ 921.35	$ 1,288.37	$ 220,757.63
60	$ 368.55	$ 919.82	$ 1,288.37	$ 220,389.08
61	$ 370.08	$ 918.29	$ 1,288.37	$ 220,019.00
62	$ 371.62	$ 916.75	$ 1,288.37	$ 219,647.38
63	$ 373.17	$ 915.20	$ 1,288.37	$ 219,274.21

PMT	PRINCIPAL	INTEREST	Total Payment	BALANCE
64	$ 374.73	$ 913.64	$ 1,288.37	$ 218,899.48
65	$ 376.29	$ 912.08	$ 1,288.37	$ 218,523.19
66	$ 377.86	$ 910.51	$ 1,288.37	$ 218,145.33
67	$ 379.43	$ 908.94	$ 1,288.37	$ 217,765.90
68	$ 381.01	$ 907.36	$ 1,288.37	$ 217,384.89
69	$ 382.60	$ 905.77	$ 1,288.37	$ 217,002.29
70	$ 384.19	$ 904.18	$ 1,288.37	$ 216,618.10
71	$ 385.79	$ 902.58	$ 1,288.37	$ 216,232.31
72	$ 387.40	$ 900.97	$ 1,288.37	$ 215,844.91
73	$ 389.02	$ 899.35	$ 1,288.37	$ 215,455.89
74	$ 390.64	$ 897.73	$ 1,288.37	$ 215,065.25
75	$ 392.26	$ 896.11	$ 1,288.37	$ 214,672.99
76	$ 393.90	$ 894.47	$ 1,288.37	$ 214,279.09
77	$ 395.54	$ 892.83	$ 1,288.37	$ 213,883.55
78	$ 397.19	$ 891.18	$ 1,288.37	$ 213,486.36
79	$ 398.84	$ 889.53	$ 1,288.37	$ 213,087.52
80	$ 400.51	$ 887.86	$ 1,288.37	$ 212,687.01
81	$ 402.17	$ 886.20	$ 1,288.37	$ 212,284.84
82	$ 403.85	$ 884.52	$ 1,288.37	$ 211,880.99
83	$ 405.53	$ 882.84	$ 1,288.37	$ 211,475.46
84	$ 407.22	$ 881.15	$ 1,288.37	$ 211,068.24
85	$ 408.92	$ 879.45	$ 1,288.37	$ 210,659.32
86	$ 410.62	$ 877.75	$ 1,288.37	$ 210,248.70
87	$ 412.33	$ 876.04	$ 1,288.37	$ 209,836.37
88	$ 414.05	$ 874.32	$ 1,288.37	$ 209,422.32
89	$ 415.78	$ 872.59	$ 1,288.37	$ 209,006.54
90	$ 417.51	$ 870.86	$ 1,288.37	$ 208,589.03
91	$ 419.25	$ 869.12	$ 1,288.37	$ 208,169.78

PMT	PRINCIPAL	INTEREST	Total Payment	BALANCE
92	$ 421.00	$ 867.37	$ 1,288.37	$ 207,748.78
93	$ 422.75	$ 865.62	$ 1,288.37	$ 207,326.03
94	$ 424.51	$ 863.86	$ 1,288.37	$ 206,901.52
95	$ 426.28	$ 862.09	$ 1,288.37	$ 206,475.24
96	$ 428.06	$ 860.31	$ 1,288.37	$ 206,047.18
97	$ 429.84	$ 858.53	$ 1,288.37	$ 205,617.34
98	$ 431.63	$ 856.74	$ 1,288.37	$ 205,185.71
99	$ 433.43	$ 854.94	$ 1,288.37	$ 204,752.28
100	$ 435.24	$ 853.13	$ 1,288.37	$ 204,317.04
101	$ 437.05	$ 851.32	$ 1,288.37	$ 203,879.99
102	$ 438.87	$ 849.50	$ 1,288.37	$ 203,441.12
103	$ 440.70	$ 847.67	$ 1,288.37	$ 203,000.42
104	$ 442.53	$ 845.84	$ 1,288.37	$ 202,557.89
105	$ 444.38	$ 843.99	$ 1,288.37	$ 202,113.51
106	$ 446.23	$ 842.14	$ 1,288.37	$ 201,667.28
107	$ 448.09	$ 840.28	$ 1,288.37	$ 201,219.19
108	$ 449.96	$ 838.41	$ 1,288.37	$ 200,769.23
109	$ 451.83	$ 836.54	$ 1,288.37	$ 200,317.40
110	$ 453.71	$ 834.66	$ 1,288.37	$ 199,863.69
111	$ 455.60	$ 832.77	$ 1,288.37	$ 199,408.09
112	$ 457.50	$ 830.87	$ 1,288.37	$ 198,950.59
113	$ 459.41	$ 828.96	$ 1,288.37	$ 198,491.18
114	$ 461.32	$ 827.05	$ 1,288.37	$ 198,029.86
115	$ 463.25	$ 825.12	$ 1,288.37	$ 197,566.61
116	$ 465.18	$ 823.19	$ 1,288.37	$ 197,101.43
117	$ 467.11	$ 821.26	$ 1,288.37	$ 196,634.32
118	$ 469.06	$ 819.31	$ 1,288.37	$ 196,165.26
119	$ 471.01	$ 817.36	$ 1,288.37	$ 195,694.25

PMT	PRINCIPAL	INTEREST	Total Payment	BALANCE
120	$ 472.98	$ 815.39	$ 1,288.37	$ 195,221.27
121	$ 474.95	$ 813.42	$ 1,288.37	$ 194,746.32
122	$ 476.93	$ 811.44	$ 1,288.37	$ 194,269.39
123	$ 478.91	$ 809.46	$ 1,288.37	$ 193,790.48
124	$ 480.91	$ 807.46	$ 1,288.37	$ 193,309.57
125	$ 482.91	$ 805.46	$ 1,288.37	$ 192,826.66
126	$ 484.93	$ 803.44	$ 1,288.37	$ 192,341.73
127	$ 486.95	$ 801.42	$ 1,288.37	$ 191,854.78
128	$ 488.98	$ 799.39	$ 1,288.37	$ 191,365.80
129	$ 491.01	$ 797.36	$ 1,288.37	$ 190,874.79
130	$ 493.06	$ 795.31	$ 1,288.37	$ 190,381.73
131	$ 495.11	$ 793.26	$ 1,288.37	$ 189,886.62
132	$ 497.18	$ 791.19	$ 1,288.37	$ 189,389.44
133	$ 499.25	$ 789.12	$ 1,288.37	$ 188,890.19
134	$ 501.33	$ 787.04	$ 1,288.37	$ 188,388.86
135	$ 503.42	$ 784.95	$ 1,288.37	$ 187,885.44
136	$ 505.51	$ 782.86	$ 1,288.37	$ 187,379.93
137	$ 507.62	$ 780.75	$ 1,288.37	$ 186,872.31
138	$ 509.74	$ 778.63	$ 1,288.37	$ 186,362.57
139	$ 511.86	$ 776.51	$ 1,288.37	$ 185,850.71
140	$ 513.99	$ 774.38	$ 1,288.37	$ 185,336.72
141	$ 516.13	$ 772.24	$ 1,288.37	$ 184,820.59
142	$ 518.28	$ 770.09	$ 1,288.37	$ 184,302.31
143	$ 520.44	$ 767.93	$ 1,288.37	$ 183,781.87
144	$ 522.61	$ 765.76	$ 1,288.37	$ 183,259.26
145	$ 524.79	$ 763.58	$ 1,288.37	$ 182,734.47
146	$ 526.98	$ 761.39	$ 1,288.37	$ 182,207.49
147	$ 529.17	$ 759.20	$ 1,288.37	$ 181,678.32

PMT	PRINCIPAL	INTEREST	Total Payment	BALANCE
148	$ 531.38	$ 756.99	$ 1,288.37	$ 181,146.94
149	$ 533.59	$ 754.78	$ 1,288.37	$ 180,613.35
150	$ 535.81	$ 752.56	$ 1,288.37	$ 180,077.54
151	$ 538.05	$ 750.32	$ 1,288.37	$ 179,539.49
152	$ 540.29	$ 748.08	$ 1,288.37	$ 178,999.20
153	$ 542.54	$ 745.83	$ 1,288.37	$ 178,456.66
154	$ 544.80	$ 743.57	$ 1,288.37	$ 177,911.86
155	$ 547.07	$ 741.30	$ 1,288.37	$ 177,364.79
156	$ 549.35	$ 739.02	$ 1,288.37	$ 176,815.44
157	$ 551.64	$ 736.73	$ 1,288.37	$ 176,263.80
158	$ 553.94	$ 734.43	$ 1,288.37	$ 175,709.86
159	$ 556.25	$ 732.12	$ 1,288.37	$ 175,153.61
160	$ 558.56	$ 729.81	$ 1,288.37	$ 174,595.05
161	$ 560.89	$ 727.48	$ 1,288.37	$ 174,034.16
162	$ 563.23	$ 725.14	$ 1,288.37	$ 173,470.93
163	$ 565.57	$ 722.80	$ 1,288.37	$ 172,905.36
164	$ 567.93	$ 720.44	$ 1,288.37	$ 172,337.43
165	$ 570.30	$ 718.07	$ 1,288.37	$ 171,767.13
166	$ 572.67	$ 715.70	$ 1,288.37	$ 171,194.46
167	$ 575.06	$ 713.31	$ 1,288.37	$ 170,619.40
168	$ 577.46	$ 710.91	$ 1,288.37	$ 170,041.94
169	$ 579.86	$ 708.51	$ 1,288.37	$ 169,462.08
170	$ 582.28	$ 706.09	$ 1,288.37	$ 168,879.80
171	$ 584.70	$ 703.67	$ 1,288.37	$ 168,295.10
172	$ 587.14	$ 701.23	$ 1,288.37	$ 167,707.96
173	$ 589.59	$ 698.78	$ 1,288.37	$ 167,118.37
174	$ 592.04	$ 696.33	$ 1,288.37	$ 166,526.33
175	$ 594.51	$ 693.86	$ 1,288.37	$ 165,931.82

PMT	PRINCIPAL	INTEREST	Total Payment	BALANCE
176	$ 596.99	$ 691.38	$ 1,288.37	$ 165,334.83
177	$ 599.47	$ 688.90	$ 1,288.37	$ 164,735.36
178	$ 601.97	$ 686.40	$ 1,288.37	$ 164,133.39
179	$ 604.48	$ 683.89	$ 1,288.37	$ 163,528.91
180	$ 607.00	$ 681.37	$ 1,288.37	$ 162,921.91
181	$ 609.53	$ 678.84	$ 1,288.37	$ 162,312.38
182	$ 612.07	$ 676.30	$ 1,288.37	$ 161,700.31
183	$ 614.62	$ 673.75	$ 1,288.37	$ 161,085.69
184	$ 617.18	$ 671.19	$ 1,288.37	$ 160,468.51
185	$ 619.75	$ 668.62	$ 1,288.37	$ 159,848.76
186	$ 622.33	$ 666.04	$ 1,288.37	$ 159,226.43
187	$ 624.93	$ 663.44	$ 1,288.37	$ 158,601.50
188	$ 627.53	$ 660.84	$ 1,288.37	$ 157,973.97
189	$ 630.15	$ 658.22	$ 1,288.37	$ 157,343.82
190	$ 632.77	$ 655.60	$ 1,288.37	$ 156,711.05
191	$ 635.41	$ 652.96	$ 1,288.37	$ 156,075.64
192	$ 638.05	$ 650.32	$ 1,288.37	$ 155,437.59
193	$ 640.71	$ 647.66	$ 1,288.37	$ 154,796.88
194	$ 643.38	$ 644.99	$ 1,288.37	$ 154,153.50
195	$ 646.06	$ 642.31	$ 1,288.37	$ 153,507.44
196	$ 648.76	$ 639.61	$ 1,288.37	$ 152,858.68
197	$ 651.46	$ 636.91	$ 1,288.37	$ 152,207.22
198	$ 654.17	$ 634.20	$ 1,288.37	$ 151,553.05
199	$ 656.90	$ 631.47	$ 1,288.37	$ 150,896.15
200	$ 659.64	$ 628.73	$ 1,288.37	$ 150,236.51
201	$ 662.38	$ 625.99	$ 1,288.37	$ 149,574.13
202	$ 665.14	$ 623.23	$ 1,288.37	$ 148,908.99
203	$ 667.92	$ 620.45	$ 1,288.37	$ 148,241.07

PMT	PRINCIPAL	INTEREST	Total Payment	BALANCE
204	$ 670.70	$ 617.67	$ 1,288.37	$ 147,570.37
205	$ 673.49	$ 614.88	$ 1,288.37	$ 146,896.88
206	$ 676.30	$ 612.07	$ 1,288.37	$ 146,220.58
207	$ 679.12	$ 609.25	$ 1,288.37	$ 145,541.46
208	$ 681.95	$ 606.42	$ 1,288.37	$ 144,859.51
209	$ 384.79	$ 603.58	$ 988.37	$ 144,174.72
210	$ 687.64	$ 600.73	$ 1,288.37	$ 143,487.08
211	$ 690.51	$ 597.86	$ 1,288.37	$ 142,796.57
212	$ 693.38	$ 594.99	$ 1,288.37	$ 142,103.19
213	$ 696.27	$ 592.10	$ 1,288.37	$ 141,406.92
214	$ 699.17	$ 589.20	$ 1,288.37	$ 140,707.75
215	$ 702.09	$ 586.28	$ 1,288.37	$ 140,005.66
216	$ 705.01	$ 583.36	$ 1,288.37	$ 139,300.65
217	$ 707.95	$ 580.42	$ 1,288.37	$ 138,592.70
218	$ 710.90	$ 577.47	$ 1,288.37	$ 137,881.80
219	$ 713.86	$ 574.51	$ 1,288.37	$ 137,167.94
220	$ 716.84	$ 571.53	$ 1,288.37	$ 136,451.10
221	$ 719.82	$ 568.55	$ 1,288.37	$ 135,731.28
222	$ 722.82	$ 565.55	$ 1,288.37	$ 135,008.46
223	$ 725.83	$ 562.54	$ 1,288.37	$ 134,282.63
224	$ 728.86	$ 559.51	$ 1,288.37	$ 133,553.77
225	$ 731.90	$ 556.47	$ 1,288.37	$ 132,821.87
226	$ 734.95	$ 553.42	$ 1,288.37	$ 132,086.92
227	$ 738.01	$ 550.36	$ 1,288.37	$ 131,348.91
228	$ 741.08	$ 547.29	$ 1,288.37	$ 130,607.83
229	$ 744.17	$ 544.20	$ 1,288.37	$ 129,863.66
230	$ 747.27	$ 541.10	$ 1,288.37	$ 129,116.39
231	$ 750.39	$ 537.98	$ 1,288.37	$ 128,366.00

PMT	PRINCIPAL	INTEREST	Total Payment	BALANCE
232	$ 753.51	$ 534.86	$ 1,288.37	$ 127,612.49
233	$ 756.65	$ 531.72	$ 1,288.37	$ 126,855.84
234	$ 759.80	$ 528.57	$ 1,288.37	$ 126,096.04
235	$ 762.97	$ 525.40	$ 1,288.37	$ 125,333.07
236	$ 766.15	$ 522.22	$ 1,288.37	$ 124,566.92
237	$ 769.34	$ 519.03	$ 1,288.37	$ 123,797.58
238	$ 772.55	$ 515.82	$ 1,288.37	$ 123,025.03
239	$ 775.77	$ 512.60	$ 1,288.37	$ 122,249.26
240	$ 779.00	$ 509.37	$ 1,288.37	$ 121,470.26
241	$ 782.24	$ 506.13	$ 1,288.37	$ 120,688.02
242	$ 785.50	$ 502.87	$ 1,288.37	$ 119,902.52
243	$ 788.78	$ 499.59	$ 1,288.37	$ 119,113.74
244	$ 792.06	$ 496.31	$ 1,288.37	$ 118,321.68
245	$ 795.36	$ 493.01	$ 1,288.37	$ 117,526.32
246	$ 798.68	$ 489.69	$ 1,288.37	$ 116,727.64
247	$ 802.00	$ 486.37	$ 1,288.37	$ 115,925.64
248	$ 805.35	$ 483.02	$ 1,288.37	$ 115,120.29
249	$ 808.70	$ 479.67	$ 1,288.37	$ 114,311.59
250	$ 812.07	$ 476.30	$ 1,288.37	$ 113,499.52
251	$ 815.46	$ 472.91	$ 1,288.37	$ 112,684.06
252	$ 818.85	$ 469.52	$ 1,288.37	$ 111,865.21
253	$ 822.26	$ 466.11	$ 1,288.37	$ 111,042.95
254	$ 825.69	$ 462.68	$ 1,288.37	$ 110,217.26
255	$ 829.13	$ 459.24	$ 1,288.37	$ 109,388.13
256	$ 832.59	$ 455.78	$ 1,288.37	$ 108,555.54
257	$ 836.06	$ 452.31	$ 1,288.37	$ 107,719.48
258	$ 839.54	$ 448.83	$ 1,288.37	$ 106,897.94
259	$ 843.04	$ 445.33	$ 1,288.37	$ 160,036.90

PMT	PRINCIPAL	INTEREST	Total Payment	BALANCE
260	$ 846.55	$ 441.82	$ 1,288.37	$ 105,190.35
261	$ 850.08	$ 438.29	$ 1,288.37	$ 104,340.27
262	$ 853.62	$ 434.75	$ 1,288.37	$ 103,486.65
263	$ 857.18	$ 431.19	$ 1,288.37	$ 102,629.47
264	$ 860.75	$ 427.62	$ 1,288.37	$ 101,768.72
265	$ 864.33	$ 424.04	$ 1,288.37	$ 100,904.39
266	$ 867.94	$ 420.43	$ 1,288.37	$ 100,036.45
267	$ 871.55	$ 416.82	$ 1,288.37	$ 99,164.90
268	$ 875.18	$ 413.19	$ 1,288.37	$ 98,289.72
269	$ 878.83	$ 409.54	$ 1,288.37	$ 97,410.89
270	$ 882.49	$ 405.88	$ 1,288.37	$ 96,528.40
271	$ 886.17	$ 402.20	$ 1,288.37	$ 95,642.23
272	$ 889.86	$ 398.51	$ 1,288.37	$ 94,752.37
273	$ 893.57	$ 394.80	$ 1,288.37	$ 93,858.80
274	$ 897.29	$ 391.08	$ 1,288.37	$ 92,961.51
275	$ 901.03	$ 387.34	$ 1,288.37	$ 92,060.48
276	$ 904.78	$ 383.59	$ 1,288.37	$ 91,155.70
277	$ 908.55	$ 379.82	$ 1,288.37	$ 90,247.15
278	$ 912.34	$ 376.02	$ 1,288.36	$ 89,334.81
279	$ 916.14	$ 372.23	$ 1,288.37	$ 88,418.67
280	$ 919.96	$ 368.41	$ 1,288.37	$ 87,498.71
281	$ 923.79	$ 364.58	$ 1,288.37	$ 86,574.92
282	$ 927.64	$ 360.73	$ 1,288.37	$ 85,647.28
283	$ 931.51	$ 356.86	$ 1,288.37	$ 84,715.77
284	$ 935.39	$ 352.98	$ 1,288.37	$ 83,780.38
285	$ 939.29	$ 349.08	$ 1,288.37	$ 82,841.09
286	$ 943.20	$ 345.17	$ 1,288.37	$ 81,897.89
287	$ 947.13	$ 341.24	$ 1,288.37	$ 80,950.76

A Collection of Thoughts

PMT	PRINCIPAL	INTEREST	Total Payment	BALANCE
288	$ 951.08	$ 337.29	$ 1,288.37	$ 79,999.68
289	$ 955.04	$ 333.33	$ 1,288.37	$ 79,044.64
290	$ 959.02	$ 329.85	$ 1,288.87	$ 78,085.62
291	$ 963.01	$ 325.36	$ 1,288.37	$ 77,122.61
292	$ 967.03	$ 321.34	$ 1,288.37	$ 76,155.58
293	$ 971.06	$ 317.31	$ 1,288.37	$ 75,184.52
294	$ 975.10	$ 313.27	$ 1,288.37	$ 74,209.42
295	$ 979.16	$ 309.21	$ 1,288.37	$ 73,230.26
296	$ 983.24	$ 305.13	$ 1,288.37	$ 72,247.02
297	$ 987.34	$ 301.03	$ 1,288.37	$ 71,259.68
298	$ 991.45	$ 296.92	$ 1,288.37	$ 70,268.23
299	$ 995.59	$ 292.78	$ 1,288.37	$ 69,272.64
300	$ 999.73	$ 286.64	$ 1,286.37	$ 68,272.91
301	$ 1,003.90	$ 284.47	$ 1,288.37	$ 67,269.01
302	$ 1,008.08	$ 280.29	$ 1,288.37	$ 66,260.93
303	$ 1,012.28	$ 276.09	$ 1,288.37	$ 65,248.65
304	$ 1,016.50	$ 271.87	$ 1,288.37	$ 64,232.15
305	$ 1,020.74	$ 267.63	$ 1,288.37	$ 63,211.41
306	$ 1,024.99	$ 263.38	$ 1,288.37	$ 62,186.42
307	$ 1,029.26	$ 259.11	$ 1,288.37	$ 61,157.16
308	$ 1,033.55	$ 254.82	$ 1,288.37	$ 60,123.61
309	$ 1,037.85	$ 250.52	$ 1,288.37	$ 59,085.76
310	$ 1,042.18	$ 246.19	$ 1,288.37	$ 58,043.58
311	$ 1,046.52	$ 241.85	$ 1,288.37	$ 56,997.06
312	$ 1,050.88	$ 237.49	$ 1,288.37	$ 55,946.18
313	$ 1,055.26	$ 233.11	$ 1,288.37	$ 54,890.92
314	$ 1,059.66	$ 228.71	$ 1,288.37	$ 53,831.26
315	$ 1,064.07	$ 224.30	$ 1,288.37	$ 52,767.19

PMT	PRINCIPAL	INTEREST	Total Payment	BALANCE
316	$ 1,068.51	$ 219.86	$ 1,288.37	$ 51,698.68
317	$ 1,072.96	$ 215.41	$ 1,288.37	$ 50,625.72
318	$ 1,077.43	$ 210.94	$ 1,288.37	$ 79,548.29
319	$ 1,081.92	$ 206.45	$ 1,288.37	$ 48,466.37
320	$ 1,086.43	$ 201.94	$ 1,288.37	$ 47,379.94
321	$ 1,090.95	$ 197.42	$ 1,288.37	$ 46,288.99
322	$ 1,095.50	$ 192.87	$ 1,288.37	$ 45,193.49
323	$ 1,100.06	$ 188.31	$ 1,288.37	$ 44,093.43
324	$ 1,104.65	$ 183.72	$ 1,288.37	$ 42,988.78
325	$ 1,109.25	$ 179.12	$ 1,288.37	$ 41,879.53
326	$ 1,113.87	$ 174.50	$ 1,288.37	$ 40,765.66
327	$ 1,118.51	$ 169.86	$ 1,288.37	$ 39,647.15
328	$ 1,123.17	$ 165.20	$ 1,288.37	$ 38,523.98
329	$ 1,127.85	$ 160.62	$ 1,288.47	$ 37,396.13
330	$ 1,132.55	$ 155.82	$ 1,288.37	$ 36,263.58
331	$ 1,137.27	$ 151.10	$ 1,288.37	$ 35,126.31
332	$ 1,142.01	$ 146.36	$ 1,288.37	$ 33,984.30
333	$ 1,146.77	$ 141.60	$ 1,288.37	$ 32,837.53
334	$ 1,151.55	$ 136.82	$ 1,288.37	$ 31,685.98
335	$ 1,156.35	$ 132.02	$ 1,288.37	$ 30,529.63
336	$ 1,161.16	$ 127.21	$ 1,288.37	$ 29,368.47
337	$ 1,166.00	$ 122.37	$ 1,288.37	$ 28,202.47
338	$ 1,170.86	$ 117.51	$ 1,288.37	$ 27,031.61
339	$ 1,175.74	$ 112.63	$ 1,288.37	$ 25,855.87
340	$ 1,180.64	$ 107.73	$ 1,288.37	$ 24,675.23
341	$ 1,185.56	$ 102.81	$ 1,288.37	$ 23,489.67
342	$ 1,190.50	$ 97.87	$ 1,288.37	$ 22,299.17
343	$ 1,195.46	$ 92.91	$ 1,288.37	$ 21,103.71

A Collection of Thoughts

PMT	PRINCIPAL	INTEREST	Total Payment	BALANCE
344	$ 1,200.44	$ 87.93	$ 1,288.37	$ 19,903.27
345	$ 1,205.44	$ 82.93	$ 1,288.37	$ 18,697.83
346	$ 1,210.46	$ 77.91	$ 1,288.37	$ 17,487.37
347	$ 1,215.51	$ 72.86	$ 1,288.37	$ 16,271.86
348	$ 1,220.57	$ 67.80	$ 1,288.37	$ 15,051.29
349	$ 1,225.66	$ 62.71	$ 1,288.37	$ 13,825.63
350	$ 1,230.76	$ 57.61	$ 1,288.37	$ 12,594.87
351	$ 1,235.89	$ 52.48	$ 1,288.37	$ 11,358.98
352	$ 1,241.04	$ 47.33	$ 1,288.37	$ 10,117.94
353	$ 1,246.21	$ 42.16	$ 1,288.37	$ 8,871.73
354	$ 1,251.40	$ 36.97	$ 1,288.37	$ 7,620.33
355	$ 1,256.62	$ 31.75	$ 1,288.37	$ 6,363.71
356	$ 1,261.85	$ 26.52	$ 1,288.37	$ 5,101.86
357	$ 1,267.11	$ 21.26	$ 1,288.37	$ 3,834.75
358	$ 1,272.39	$ 15.98	$ 1,288.37	$ 2,562.36
359	$ 1,277.69	$ 10.68	$ 1,288.37	$ 1,284.67
360	$ 1,584.67	$ 5.35	$ 1,590.02	$ -
Totals	$ 240,000.00	$ 223,813.44	$ 463,813.44	

15-Year Mortgage

- Buy a $300,000 home.
- Put 20% down or $60,000.
- This leaves a $240,000 mortgage, spread over 180 equal monthly payments.
- Fixed Interest Rate is 4.0%. Banks will give you a lower interest rate in exchange for the loan being paid off quicker.
- Note the total interest paid of $79,544 at the bottom of this schedule. Thus, **the $240,000 loan actually costs you $319,544**.
- Lesson learned: By paying the same house off in 15 years versus 30 years, **we saved $144,269**.

PMT	PRINCIPAL	INTEREST	Total Payment	BALANCE
1	$ 975.25	$ 800.00	$ 1,775.25	$ 239,024.75
2	$ 978.50	$ 796.75	$ 1,775.25	$ 238,046.25
3	$ 981.76	$ 793.49	$ 1,775.25	$ 237,064.49
4	$ 985.04	$ 790.21	$ 1,775.25	$ 236,079.45
5	$ 988.32	$ 786.93	$ 1,775.25	$ 235,091.13
6	$ 991.61	$ 783.64	$ 1,775.25	$ 234,099.52
7	$ 994.92	$ 780.33	$ 1,775.25	$ 233,104.60
8	$ 998.23	$ 777.02	$ 1,775.25	$ 232,106.37
9	$ 1,001.56	$ 773.69	$ 1,775.25	$ 231,104.81
10	$ 1,004.90	$ 770.35	$ 1,775.25	$ 230,099.91
11	$ 1,008.25	$ 767.00	$ 1,775.25	$ 229,091.66
12	$ 1,011.61	$ 763.64	$ 1,775.25	$ 228,080.05
13	$ 1,014.98	$ 760.27	$ 1,775.25	$ 227,065.07
14	$ 1,018.37	$ 756.88	$ 1,775.25	$ 226,046.70
15	$ 1,021.76	$ 753.49	$ 1,775.25	$ 225,024.94

PMT	PRINCIPAL	INTEREST	Total Payment	BALANCE
16	$ 1,025.17	$ 750.08	$ 1,775.25	$ 223,999.77
17	$ 1,028.58	$ 746.67	$ 1,775.25	$ 222,971.19
18	$ 1,032.01	$ 743.24	$ 1,775.25	$ 221,939.18
19	$ 1,035.45	$ 739.80	$ 1,775.25	$ 220,903.73
20	$ 1,038.90	$ 736.35	$ 1,775.25	$ 219,864.83
21	$ 1,042.37	$ 732.88	$ 1,775.25	$ 218,822.46
22	$ 1,045.84	$ 729.41	$ 1,775.25	$ 217,776.62
23	$ 1,049.33	$ 725.92	$ 1,775.25	$ 216,727.29
24	$ 1,052.83	$ 722.42	$ 1,775.25	$ 215,674.46
25	$ 1,056.34	$ 718.91	$ 1,775.25	$ 214,618.12
26	$ 1,059.86	$ 715.39	$ 1,775.25	$ 213,558.26
27	$ 1,063.39	$ 711.86	$ 1,775.25	$ 212,494.87
28	$ 1,066.93	$ 708.32	$ 1,775.25	$ 211,427.94
29	$ 1,070.49	$ 704.76	$ 1,775.25	$ 210,357.45
30	$ 1,074.06	$ 701.19	$ 1,775.25	$ 209,283.39
31	$ 1,077.64	$ 697.61	$ 1,775.25	$ 208,205.75
32	$ 1,081.23	$ 694.02	$ 1,775.25	$ 207,124.52
33	$ 1,084.83	$ 690.42	$ 1,775.25	$ 206,039.69
34	$ 1,088.45	$ 686.40	$ 1,774.85	$ 204,951.24
35	$ 1,092.08	$ 683.17	$ 1,775.25	$ 203,859.16
36	$ 1,095.72	$ 679.53	$ 1,775.25	$ 202,763.44
37	$ 1,099.37	$ 675.88	$ 1,775.25	$ 201,664.07
38	$ 1,103.04	$ 672.21	$ 1,775.25	$ 200,561.03
39	$ 1,106.71	$ 668.54	$ 1,775.25	$ 199,454.32
40	$ 1,110.40	$ 664.85	$ 1,775.25	$ 198,343.92
41	$ 1,114.10	$ 661.15	$ 1,775.25	$ 197,229.82
42	$ 1,117.82	$ 657.43	$ 1,775.25	$ 196,112.00
43	$ 1,121.54	$ 653.71	$ 1,775.25	$ 194,990.46

PMT	PRINCIPAL	INTEREST	Total Payment	BALANCE
44	$ 1,125.28	$ 649.97	$ 1,775.25	$ 193,865.18
45	$ 1,129.03	$ 646.22	$ 1,775.25	$ 192,736.15
46	$ 1,132.80	$ 642.45	$ 1,775.25	$ 191,603.35
47	$ 1,136.57	$ 638.68	$ 1,775.25	$ 190,466.78
48	$ 1,140.36	$ 634.89	$ 1,775.25	$ 189,326.42
49	$ 1,144.16	$ 631.09	$ 1,775.25	$ 188,182.26
50	$ 1,147.98	$ 627.27	$ 1,775.25	$ 187,034.28
51	$ 1,151.80	$ 623.45	$ 1,775.25	$ 185,882.48
52	$ 1,155.64	$ 619.61	$ 1,775.25	$ 184,726.84
53	$ 1,159.47	$ 615.76	$ 1,775.23	$ 183,567.35
54	$ 1,163.36	$ 611.89	$ 1,775.25	$ 182,403.99
55	$ 1,167.24	$ 608.01	$ 1,775.25	$ 181,236.75
56	$ 1,171.13	$ 604.12	$ 1,775.25	$ 180,065.62
57	$ 1,175.03	$ 600.22	$ 1,775.25	$ 178,890.59
58	$ 1,178.95	$ 596.30	$ 1,775.25	$ 177,711.64
59	$ 1,182.88	$ 592.37	$ 1,775.25	$ 176,528.76
60	$ 1,186.82	$ 588.43	$ 1,775.25	$ 175,341.94
61	$ 1,190.78	$ 584.47	$ 1,775.25	$ 174,151.16
62	$ 1,194.75	$ 580.50	$ 1,775.25	$ 172,956.41
63	$ 1,198.73	$ 576.52	$ 1,775.25	$ 171,757.68
64	$ 1,202.72	$ 572.53	$ 1,775.25	$ 170,554.96
65	$ 1,206.73	$ 568.52	$ 1,775.25	$ 169,348.23
66	$ 1,210.76	$ 564.49	$ 1,775.25	$ 168,137.47
67	$ 1,214.79	$ 560.46	$ 1,775.25	$ 166,922.68
68	$ 1,218.84	$ 556.41	$ 1,775.25	$ 165,703.84
69	$ 1,222.90	$ 552.35	$ 1,775.25	$ 164,480.94
70	$ 1,226.98	$ 548.27	$ 1,775.25	$ 163,253.96
71	$ 1,231.07	$ 544.18	$ 1,775.25	$ 162,022.89

PMT	PRINCIPAL	INTEREST	Total Payment	BALANCE
72	$ 1,235.17	$ 540.08	$ 1,775.25	$ 160,787.72
73	$ 1,239.29	$ 535.96	$ 1,775.25	$ 159,548.43
74	$ 1,243.42	$ 531.83	$ 1,775.25	$ 158,305.01
75	$ 1,247.57	$ 527.68	$ 1,775.25	$ 157,057.44
76	$ 1,251.73	$ 523.52	$ 1,775.25	$ 155,805.71
77	$ 1,255.90	$ 519.35	$ 1,775.25	$ 154,549.81
78	$ 1,260.08	$ 515.17	$ 1,775.25	$ 153,289.73
79	$ 1,264.28	$ 510.97	$ 1,775.25	$ 152,025.45
80	$ 1,268.50	$ 506.75	$ 1,775.25	$ 150,756.95
81	$ 1,272.73	$ 502.52	$ 1,775.25	$ 149,484.22
82	$ 1,276.97	$ 498.28	$ 1,775.25	$ 148,207.25
83	$ 1,281.23	$ 494.02	$ 1,775.25	$ 146,926.02
84	$ 1,285.50	$ 489.75	$ 1,775.25	$ 145,640.52
85	$ 1,289.78	$ 485.47	$ 1,775.25	$ 144,350.74
86	$ 1,294.08	$ 481.17	$ 1,775.25	$ 143,056.66
87	$ 1,298.39	$ 476.86	$ 1,775.25	$ 141,758.27
88	$ 1,302.72	$ 472.53	$ 1,775.25	$ 140,455.55
89	$ 1,307.06	$ 468.19	$ 1,775.25	$ 139,148.49
90	$ 1,311.42	$ 463.83	$ 1,775.25	$ 137,837.07
91	$ 1,315.79	$ 459.46	$ 1,775.25	$ 136,521.28
92	$ 1,320.18	$ 455.07	$ 1,775.25	$ 135,201.10
93	$ 1,324.58	$ 450.67	$ 1,775.25	$ 133,876.52
94	$ 1,328.99	$ 446.26	$ 1,775.25	$ 132,547.53
95	$ 1,333.42	$ 441.83	$ 1,775.25	$ 131,214.11
96	$ 1,337.87	$ 437.38	$ 1,775.25	$ 129,876.24
97	$ 1,342.33	$ 432.92	$ 1,775.25	$ 128,533.91
98	$ 1,346.80	$ 428.45	$ 1,775.25	$ 127,187.11
99	$ 1,351.29	$ 423.96	$ 1,775.25	$ 125,835.82

PMT	PRINCIPAL	INTEREST	Total Payment	BALANCE
100	$ 1,355.80	$ 419.45	$ 1,775.25	$ 124,480.02
101	$ 1,360.32	$ 414.93	$ 1,775.25	$ 123,119.70
102	$ 1,364.85	$ 410.40	$ 1,775.25	$ 121,754.85
103	$ 1,369.40	$ 405.85	$ 1,775.25	$ 120,385.45
104	$ 1,373.97	$ 401.28	$ 1,775.25	$ 119,011.48
105	$ 1,378.55	$ 396.70	$ 1,775.25	$ 117,632.93
106	$ 1,383.14	$ 392.11	$ 1,775.25	$ 116,249.79
107	$ 1,387.75	$ 387.50	$ 1,775.25	$ 114,862.04
108	$ 1,392.38	$ 382.87	$ 1,775.25	$ 113,469.66
109	$ 1,397.02	$ 378.23	$ 1,775.25	$ 112,072.64
110	$ 1,401.67	$ 373.58	$ 1,775.25	$ 110,670.97
111	$ 1,405.35	$ 368.90	$ 1,774.25	$ 109,264.62
112	$ 1,411.03	$ 364.22	$ 1,775.25	$ 107,853.59
113	$ 1,415.74	$ 359.51	$ 1,775.25	$ 106,437.85
114	$ 1,420.46	$ 354.79	$ 1,775.25	$ 105,017.39
115	$ 1,425.19	$ 350.06	$ 1,775.25	$ 103,592.20
116	$ 1,429.94	$ 345.31	$ 1,775.25	$ 102,162.26
117	$ 1,434.71	$ 340.54	$ 1,775.25	$ 100,727.55
118	$ 1,439.49	$ 335.76	$ 1,775.25	$ 99,288.06
119	$ 1,444.29	$ 330.96	$ 1,775.25	$ 97,843.77
120	$ 1,449.10	$ 326.15	$ 1,775.25	$ 96,394.67
121	$ 1,453.93	$ 321.32	$ 1,775.25	$ 94,940.74
122	$ 1,458.78	$ 316.47	$ 1,775.25	$ 93,481.96
123	$ 1,463.64	$ 311.61	$ 1,775.25	$ 92,018.32
124	$ 1,468.52	$ 306.73	$ 1,775.25	$ 90,549.80
125	$ 1,473.42	$ 301.83	$ 1,775.25	$ 89,076.38
126	$ 1,478.33	$ 296.92	$ 1,775.25	$ 87,598.05
127	$ 1,483.26	$ 291.99	$ 1,775.25	$ 86,114.79

PMT	PRINCIPAL	INTEREST	Total Payment	BALANCE
128	$ 1,488.20	$ 287.05	$ 1,775.25	$ 84,626.59
129	$ 1,493.16	$ 282.09	$ 1,775.25	$ 83,133.43
130	$ 1,498.14	$ 277.11	$ 1,775.25	$ 81,635.29
131	$ 1,503.13	$ 272.12	$ 1,775.25	$ 80,132.16
132	$ 1,508.14	$ 267.11	$ 1,775.25	$ 78,624.02
133	$ 1,513.17	$ 262.08	$ 1,775.25	$ 77,110.85
134	$ 1,518.21	$ 257.04	$ 1,775.25	$ 75,592.64
135	$ 1,523.27	$ 251.98	$ 1,775.25	$ 74,069.37
136	$ 1,528.35	$ 246.90	$ 1,775.25	$ 72,541.02
137	$ 1,533.45	$ 241.80	$ 1,775.25	$ 71,007.57
138	$ 1,538.56	$ 236.69	$ 1,775.25	$ 69,469.01
139	$ 1,543.69	$ 231.56	$ 1,775.25	$ 67,925.32
140	$ 1,548.83	$ 226.42	$ 1,775.25	$ 66,376.49
141	$ 1,554.00	$ 221.25	$ 1,775.25	$ 64,822.49
142	$ 1,559.18	$ 216.07	$ 1,775.25	$ 63,263.31
143	$ 1,564.37	$ 210.88	$ 1,775.25	$ 61,698.94
144	$ 1,569.59	$ 205.66	$ 1,775.25	$ 60,129.35
145	$ 1,574.82	$ 200.43	$ 1,775.25	$ 58,554.53
146	$ 1,580.07	$ 195.18	$ 1,775.25	$ 56,974.46
147	$ 1,585.34	$ 189.91	$ 1,775.25	$ 55,389.12
148	$ 1,590.62	$ 184.63	$ 1,775.25	$ 53,798.50
149	$ 1,595.92	$ 179.33	$ 1,775.25	$ 52,202.58
150	$ 1,601.24	$ 174.01	$ 1,775.25	$ 50,601.34
151	$ 1,606.58	$ 168.67	$ 1,775.25	$ 48,994.76
152	$ 1,611.93	$ 163.32	$ 1,775.25	$ 47,382.83
153	$ 1,617.31	$ 157.94	$ 1,775.25	$ 45,765.52
154	$ 1,622.70	$ 152.55	$ 1,775.25	$ 44,142.82
155	$ 1,628.11	$ 147.14	$ 1,775.25	$ 42,514.71

PMT	PRINCIPAL	INTEREST	Total Payment	BALANCE
156	$ 1,633.53	$ 141.72	$ 1,775.25	$ 40,881.18
157	$ 1,638.98	$ 136.27	$ 1,775.25	$ 39,242.20
158	$ 1,644.44	$ 130.81	$ 1,775.25	$ 37,597.76
159	$ 1,649.92	$ 125.33	$ 1,775.25	$ 35,947.84
160	$ 1,655.42	$ 119.83	$ 1,775.25	$ 34,292.42
161	$ 1,660.94	$ 114.31	$ 1,775.25	$ 32,631.48
162	$ 1,666.48	$ 108.77	$ 1,775.25	$ 30,965.00
163	$ 1,672.03	$ 103.22	$ 1,775.25	$ 29,292.97
164	$ 1,677.61	$ 97.64	$ 1,775.25	$ 27,615.36
165	$ 1,683.20	$ 92.05	$ 1,775.25	$ 25,932.16
166	$ 1,688.81	$ 86.44	$ 1,775.25	$ 24,243.35
167	$ 1,694.44	$ 80.81	$ 1,775.25	$ 22,548.91
168	$ 1,700.09	$ 75.16	$ 1,775.25	$ 20,848.82
169	$ 1,705.75	$ 69.50	$ 1,775.25	$ 19,143.07
170	$ 1,711.44	$ 63.81	$ 1,775.25	$ 17,431.63
171	$ 1,717.14	$ 58.11	$ 1,775.25	$ 15,714.49
172	$ 1,722.87	$ 52.38	$ 1,775.25	$ 13,991.62
173	$ 1,728.61	$ 46.64	$ 1,775.25	$ 12,263.01
174	$ 1,734.37	$ 40.88	$ 1,775.25	$ 10,528.64
175	$ 1,740.15	$ 35.10	$ 1,775.25	$ 8,788.49
176	$ 1,745.96	$ 29.29	$ 1,775.25	$ 7,042.53
177	$ 1,751.77	$ 23.48	$ 1,775.25	$ 5,290.76
178	$ 1,757.61	$ 17.64	$ 1,775.25	$ 3,533.15
179	$ 1,763.47	$ 11.78	$ 1,775.25	$ 1,769.68
180	$ 1,770.70	$ 4.55	$ 1,775.25	$ -
Totals	$ 240,000.00	$ 79,543.58	$ 319,543.58	

5-Year Car Loan

- Buy a $36,000 car.
- Put 20% down or $6,000.
- This leaves a $30,000 loan, spread over 60 equal monthly payments.
- Fixed Interest Rate is 6.0%.
- Note the total interest paid of $4,769 at the bottom of this schedule. Thus, **the $30,000 loan actually costs you $34,769**.

PMT	PRINCIPAL	INTEREST	Total Payment	BALANCE
1	$ 429.98	$ 150.00	$ 579.98	$ 29,570.02
2	$ 432.13	$ 147.85	$ 579.98	$ 29,137.89
3	$ 434.29	$ 145.69	$ 579.98	$ 28,703.60
4	$ 436.46	$ 143.52	$ 579.98	$ 28,267.14
5	$ 438.64	$ 141.34	$ 579.98	$ 27,828.50
6	$ 440.84	$ 139.14	$ 579.98	$ 27,387.66
7	$ 443.04	$ 136.94	$ 579.98	$ 26,944.62
8	$ 445.26	$ 134.72	$ 579.98	$ 26,499.36
9	$ 447.48	$ 132.50	$ 579.98	$ 26,051.88
10	$ 449.72	$ 130.26	$ 579.98	$ 25,602.16
11	$ 451.97	$ 128.01	$ 579.98	$ 25,150.19
12	$ 454.23	$ 125.75	$ 579.98	$ 24,695.96
13	$ 456.50	$ 123.48	$ 579.98	$ 24,239.46
14	$ 458.78	$ 121.20	$ 579.98	$ 23,780.68
15	$ 461.08	$ 118.90	$ 579.98	$ 23,319.60
16	$ 463.38	$ 116.60	$ 579.98	$ 22,856.22
17	$ 465.70	$ 114.28	$ 579.98	$ 22,390.52
18	$ 468.03	$ 111.95	$ 579.98	$ 21,922.49

PMT	PRINCIPAL	INTEREST	Total Payment	BALANCE
19	$ 470.37	$ 109.61	$ 579.98	$ 21,452.12
20	$ 472.72	$ 107.26	$ 579.98	$ 20,979.40
21	$ 475.08	$ 104.90	$ 579.98	$ 20,504.32
22	$ 477.46	$ 102.52	$ 579.98	$ 20,026.86
23	$ 479.85	$ 100.13	$ 579.98	$ 19,547.01
24	$ 482.24	$ 97.74	$ 579.98	$ 19,064.77
25	$ 484.66	$ 95.32	$ 579.98	$ 18,580.11
26	$ 487.08	$ 92.90	$ 579.98	$ 18,093.03
27	$ 489.51	$ 90.47	$ 579.98	$ 17,603.52
28	$ 491.96	$ 88.02	$ 579.98	$ 17,111.56
29	$ 494.42	$ 85.56	$ 579.98	$ 16,617.14
30	$ 496.89	$ 83.09	$ 579.98	$ 16,120.25
31	$ 499.38	$ 80.60	$ 579.98	$ 15,620.87
32	$ 501.88	$ 78.10	$ 579.98	$ 15,118.99
33	$ 504.39	$ 75.59	$ 579.98	$ 14,614.60
34	$ 506.91	$ 73.07	$ 579.98	$ 14,107.69
35	$ 509.44	$ 70.54	$ 579.98	$ 13,598.25
36	$ 511.99	$ 67.99	$ 579.98	$ 13,086.26
37	$ 514.55	$ 35.43	$ 549.98	$ 12,571.71
38	$ 517.12	$ 62.86	$ 579.98	$ 12,054.59
39	$ 519.71	$ 60.27	$ 579.98	$ 11,534.88
40	$ 522.31	$ 57.67	$ 579.98	$ 11,012.57
41	$ 524.92	$ 55.06	$ 579.98	$ 10,487.65
42	$ 527.54	$ 52.44	$ 579.98	$ 9,960.11
43	$ 530.18	$ 49.80	$ 579.98	$ 9,429.93
44	$ 532.83	$ 47.15	$ 579.98	$ 8,897.10
45	$ 535.49	$ 44.49	$ 579.98	$ 8,361.61
46	$ 538.17	$ 41.81	$ 579.98	$ 7,823.44

PMT	PRINCIPAL	INTEREST	Total Payment	BALANCE
47	$ 540.86	$ 39.12	$ 579.98	$ 7,282.58
48	$ 543.57	$ 36.41	$ 579.98	$ 6,739.01
49	$ 546.28	$ 33.70	$ 579.98	$ 6,192.73
50	$ 549.02	$ 30.96	$ 579.98	$ 5,643.71
51	$ 551.76	$ 28.22	$ 579.98	$ 5,091.95
52	$ 554.52	$ 25.46	$ 579.98	$ 4,537.43
53	$ 557.29	$ 22.69	$ 579.98	$ 3,980.14
54	$ 560.08	$ 19.90	$ 579.98	$ 3,420.06
55	$ 562.88	$ 17.10	$ 579.98	$ 2,857.18
56	$ 565.69	$ 14.29	$ 579.98	$ 2,291.49
57	$ 568.52	$ 11.46	$ 579.98	$ 1,722.97
58	$ 571.37	$ 8.61	$ 579.98	$ 1,151.60
59	$ 574.22	$ 5.76	$ 579.98	$ 577.38
60	$ 577.38	$ 2.89	$ 580.27	$ -
Totals	$ 30,000.00	$ 4,769.09	$ 34,769.09	

ABOUT THE AUTHOR

Michael Johns has spent the last 25 years working for companies such as Xerox, EMC, and Dell Technologies, serving in various roles in the technology field: Operations, Sales, and Consulting. He's been fortunate to work with many outstanding people and has won a few awards along the way. He was inspired to become a voracious reader by his sixth-grade teacher, something that turned into a life-long habit of reading and learning. This is the first book he has written. While he never set out to become an author, having children became a calling that needed to be answered. *From a Father to a Child* is meant to be a legacy for his three children. He lives in Louisville, Kentucky, with his wife, Wendi, and their three children, Nicholas, Hayli Rose, and Noah.

For more information about Michael R. Johns and
From a Father to a Child, please visit

www.michaelrjohns.com

With every donation, a voice will be given to
the creativity that lies within the hearts of
our children living with diverse challenges.

By making this difference, children that may
not have been given the opportunity to have their
Heart Heard will have the freedom to create
beautiful works of art and musical creations.

Donate by visiting

HeartstobeHeard.com

We thank you.

Made in the USA
Columbia, SC
26 March 2022